The Home of the Learned Man

FRANZ ADLER

MARTIN GROTJAHN

JOHN KOSA

DANIEL KUBAT

ARTHUR LANGDORF

WILLIAM T. LIU

JOHN MOGEY

JOHN M. MUNRO

JULIUS REZLER

JOSEPH S. ROUCEK

SIEGFRIED WENZEL

The Home of

the Learned Man

A Symposium on the Immigrant Scholar in America

Edited by
JOHN KOSA

Foreword by
SENATOR EDWARD M. KENNEDY

COLLEGE & UNIVERSITY PRESS · *Publishers*
NEW HAVEN, CONN.

To Americans of All Nations,
This Is Dedicated.

Salvador de Madariaga, *I. Americans*

Contents

About the Authors

FRANZ ADLER was born and educated in Vienna, Austria, and is now associate professor of sociology at Los Angeles State College.

MARTIN GROTJAHN, born and educated in Berlin, Germany, is a psychiatrist working as private practitioner, training analyst and clinical professor of psychiatry at the University of Southern California.

JOHN KOSA, a Hungarian-born sociologist, is lecturer and director of the medical care research unit at Harvard Medical School.

DANIEL KUBAT left his native Czechoslovakia in 1949 and is now associate professor of sociology at the University of Florida.

ARTHUR LANGDORF is the pseudonym of a foreign-born scholar. His article was translated into English by John Kosa.

WILLIAM T. LIU, born in China and educated in the United States, is professor of sociology at the University of Notre Dame.

JOHN MOGEY was born in Ireland and is now professor and chairman of the department of sociology at Boston University.

JOHN M. MUNRO was born and educated in England, taught English in the United States and Canada, and is now on the staff of the American University, Beirut, Lebanon.

JULIUS REZLER, born in Hungary, is now professor at the Institute of Social and Industrial Relations of Loyola University, Chicago.

JOSEPH S. ROUCEK, of Czechoslovak origin, is professor of sociology at Queensborough Community College of the City University of New York.

SIEGFRIED WENZEL, born in Germany, is now assistant professor of English at the University of North Carolina.

SENATOR EDWARD M. KENNEDY

Foreword

The abundant resources of this land provided the foundation for a great nation. But only people could make the opportunity a reality. Immigration provided the human resources. More than that, it infused the nation with a commitment to far horizons and new frontiers, and thereby kept the pioneer spirit of American life, the spirit of equality and of hope, always alive and strong. "We are the heirs of all time," wrote Herman Melville, "and with all nations we divide our inheritance."*

Immigration is the oldest theme in America's history and reminds us all that the nobility to which our country has risen was born of humble origins. The immigrants came, and continue to come—creative, industrious, unafraid. Many have achieved greatness, or have risen to positions of national leadership. Many more are anonymous to the pages of history. But all have entered the fabric of our society. Their contributions are seen in the communities of all our states and in the total strength of our nation. Their mutual concern and cooperative effort in helping to build a free society is the unquestioned genius of the American experience.

Among the millions of immigrants who have come to our shores, there has always been a significant element of exceptional men. Many were scholars. Some were trained in the advanced techniques and concepts of the Old World and brought with them reservoirs of knowledge and expertise, which were so important to the development of learning in the New World. Some were individuals who, only in America's air of freedom, were able to give forceful and imaginative expression to their gifted

* John F. Kennedy, *A Nation of Immigrants*. Revised and enlarged edition (New York and Evanston: Harper and Row, 1964), p. 68.

11

minds. Some were sons of peasants and fishermen who fulfilled hopes for opportunity and freedom, and emerged into creative productivity in various fields of learning. All were individuals who enriched their adopted country.

The several essays in this volume are written by contemporary immigrant scholars. These scholars relate not only their personal experiences as immigrants and their observations on the complex and often articulate and influential role the immigrant scholar plays in American history, but they also address themselves to more substantive questions, such as the national limitations of scholarship, the important role of the United States as an international center for learning and producing knowledge, and the enormous potential for the welfare of mankind in promoting the "united scholarship" of all nations. As the editor points out in his concluding comments, it is an anachronism to measure contemporary learning in terms of "tribal wisdom or national scholarship." More and more, today's men of learning—from north to south, from east to west, throughout the world—form a single community and speak the same language, hampered in communication and the pursuit of excellence only by repressive national ideologies and restrictive political and social systems. The United States, moreover, grateful for the creativity and industriousness of its exceptional men acquired through migration, has become an international center for scholars. In addition to the relatively small numbers of scholars who emigrate annually to our country, thousands of men and women from around the world come as visitors to study and to learn in our colleges and universities, in our industrial and agricultural and commercial enterprises. The mutual benefits derived from such pursuits broaden the horizons and enrich the lives of all concerned.

Throughout history the creative productivity of scholars has been scarce and highly valued by all nations. But in the modern world, with its extraordinary pressures for progress and development, the value of the creative mind and each nation's efforts to stimulate the presence of a growing number of exceptional men within its boundaries, has taken on new significance and importance throughout the world. As a result, the emigration of the talented in recent years has generated an international problem, which in the popular vernacular is called the "brain

drain." The contributors to this volume are part of this phenomenon. The extent and significance of this international migration and the loss of talented manpower from one country
to another is a matter of growing concern within the international community. The United States, inevitably, is bearing the
brunt of protest in this area, and American immigration policy
is the object of sharp criticism from many quarters, especially
in Europe.

Since the enactment of the Immigration Act of 1965, which
abolished the national origin quota system and put in its place
a new formula based on equality and fair play for the people of
all nations, there has been a growing interest in the "brain drain"
issue within the Congress. Because of my deep personal interest
in the field of migration for the past several years, and as Acting
Chairman of the Judiciary Subcommittee on Immigration and
Naturalization, I took the initiative to have the Subcommittee
conduct an extensive inquiry into this extremely complex and
difficult problem. Various views on the nature and significance
of the "brain drain," and on the degree of responsibility which
the United States should assume in helping to ameliorate the
situation, have been presented to the Subcommittee for its consideration.

The "brain drain" phenomenon must be viewed in two dimensions. The first relates to the movement of talented persons
among advanced countries with a strong base in modern technology and education. There is little doubt that the most significant part of this movement is from Europe to the United
States, and to Canada as well. The situation is viewed by many
Europeans as a major factor contributing to the technological
gap between Europe and North America. This simple thesis,
however, is misleading. To attribute the technological gap to
the emigration of talented manpower is to ignore the causes of
emigration which lie in a historically complex pattern of institutional, managerial, political, social and cultural conditions in
many countries of Europe, conditions which often blunt the aspirations of exceptional men, inevitably causing their emigration.
In the main, these are conditions which Europeans themselves
must and can overcome. The capacity to do so is there. British
Prime Minister Harold Wilson, with whom the phrase "brain

drain" reportedly originated, summarized this attitude well a few years ago in an address to his Labor Party's Annual Conference in Scarborough. He said:

> . . . we must hold our scientists in this country. The Royal Society has recently reported that 12 per cent of the new Ph.D.s are now leaving this country every year to go abroad. We have heard recently of universities where practically the whole scientific department has emigrated en bloc. Only the other day I heard of one of our most famous scientific colleges where in one particular faculty nine Ph.D.s have been awarded this year in a field which is as relevant to the future of Britain as any subject I could think of, and of those nine, seven have already left to go to the United States. Lord Hailsham tells us that this loss of scientists is due to the deficiencies of the American educational system. His Lordship is wrong. It is due not to the deficiencies of the American educational system; it is due to the deficiencies of the British industrial system; in that we do not put a proper valuation on our trained scientists; that they are not afforded the status and the prospects to which they are entitled.
>
> I have talked in America to British scientists who have gone abroad. It is not so much a question of salary; it is the poor valuation put on their work by British industry and in some cases by impoverished British universities; the inadequate provision of adequate research facilities and equipment. It is because in so many cases in British industry today promotion for a scientist depends on waiting for dead men's shoes. Britain is not so rich in facilities for training scientists and technologists that we can let this brain drain continue. We are not even selling the seed corn, we are giving it away.

The far more dramatic and serious dimension of the "brain drain" phenomenon involves the less developed countries of the world—countries in Africa, Asia, and Latin America without a strong base, and often without any semblance thereof, in modern technology and education. These countries desperately need men of learning and trained personnel in all fields, if they are to pursue successfully the spirited adventure of national independence and social and economic development. They desperately need exceptional men—men who can lead, administer, innovate, and direct. There is little doubt the emigration of talented manpower from many of these countries to North America and Europe, and the non-return of their nationals studying abroad, inevitably tends to weaken their potential and, in some cases, may actually jeopardize their capacity for development. Again, as in the case of advanced countries adversely affected by the emigration of talented manpower, the basic responsibility for ameliorating the situation lies with the developing countries themselves.

In this connection, the loss of talent through emigration should not be viewed in isolation by the parties concerned, nor as a primary problem of the developing countries. Rather, it should be viewed as a symptom of the basic long-term problem of national development in all spheres—as an indicator of conditions which should be remedied at the source. For nothing will halt the free emigration of exceptional men from an economically weak, a politically unstable, and a socially rigid country, or from a society which denies intellectual freedom, or from a nation which fails to adopt vigorous and progressive policies for improving higher education and research and for promoting activities in which the talents of the citizenry are not used or appreciated. The so-called "brain drain," especially from the less developed areas of the world, is an important matter, therefore, because it raises in a most dramatic way the question of the kind of world in which the American people will want to live a generation or less from now. Obviously, it is a world in which the critical challenge of the gap between the rich and poor nations is being met, a world in which most nations possess the actual or near potential capacity for self-sustaining growth, and adequate intellectual resources and leadership of their own.

What is done to assist the developing countries in moderating the "brain drain" problem is, in the main, what we should be doing to raise their level of development in all areas so as to help satisfy the legitimate aspirations of their citizens and thereby contribute to the stability, progress, and peace of the world. In the final analysis, the measure of our willingness to approach positively the long-term difficulties associated with the international migration of talent and skills from the developing countries, is our willingness to support a national and multilateral effort to aid their developmental process totally. We must, however, be more generous in our assistance to those who would help themselves. Moreover, because the best hope for progress in building modern societies throughout the world lies in the expansion of the world's stock of resources, especially human resources, special efforts should be made in education and training, in manpower policy and planning. And, inevitably, the greatest growth and progress will occur under conditions of freedom, and in those nations where social justice and individual opportunity are actively pursued by responsible leaders. Democratic development in its fullness of political, social, economic, material and spiritual change, harbors a challenge that should excite Americans and generate the commitment of all peoples.

It is in meeting this long-term challenge, rather than in the immediate placing of arbitrary restraints on the freedom of movement, as some would suggest, that an answer will finally be found to the international problem called "brain drain." This should not imply in the meantime, however, a laissez-faire and unrestrained competitive market for the exceptional man between the United States, for example, and the developing countries. In addition to our over-all efforts to help meet the long-term challenge of modernization, we must also recognize the immediately adverse effects of emigration upon specific developing countries, and do what we can to assist them in retaining their exceptional men. Through our governmental and private facilities we must also encourage visitors to our shores to return to their homelands and utilize their acquired knowledge in the interest of their country's development. But nothing we do should obviate the *opportunity* of free movement. Freedom of movement, including movement from one country to another, is, in fact, a basic principle of the democratic faith. Moreover, there is little doubt that the long-term benefits accruing to the world from the circulation of brains, is, with few exceptions, far greater than the immediate adverse effects of a country's losing a scholar through emigration or the choice of one of its students abroad to remain outside his homeland. The international tradition established at universities in Bologna, Paris, Oxford, and elsewhere, where all scholars were welcome on a temporary or permanent basis, has served the cause of human progress well. History clearly demonstrates that the contributions of exceptional men, in whatever field or country they work, are not confined within national boundaries, but usually serve to advance productivity and human welfare throughout the world.

And so, in helping to meet the challenge of modernizing the planet, we must strive to keep open opportunities of free movement with their commitments "to far horizons and new frontiers." In the long run, we must strive for an even greater circulation of talented men and women, and fully explore the enormous potential for the welfare of mankind in promoting the "united scholarship" of all nations.

Preface

IN MOMENTS of a transcendental mood we are prone to think of knowledge as something ethereal that is present everywhere in the same substance and form and spreads unhindered over borders, fences, and obstacles erected by man. In such moments it feels outright embarrassing to think of the geographical limitations of learning—and yet, the facts cannot be denied. In a less spiritual mood we have to admit that learning is much like hard money: it is amassed in certain places and conspicuously lacking in others.

Here is the case of America with her monetary and scholastic wealth apparent to any observer. And here is the case of the immigrant scholar, a ubiquitous figure in America, who has come from almost any country (some of them evidently lacking in scholastic wealth) to work on our campuses, in our research institutes and any other place where knowledge is produced or put to some use. Is this conspicuous hoarding of learned men by the wealthiest country of the world just a matter of economic laws, just the purchase of the best brainpower available on the international market? Or is it a matter of more emotional nature, a matter of America, the country of all nations, offering a new home to the learned man of any birth?

Having seen migrants and refugees, learned and unlearned, far beyond any count, I may ask: Where is the home of the learned man? How much settled does the immigrant scholar feel in this country? By all evidence he fits into the place that he happens to occupy in the scholarly enterprise of the nation, but at the same time he is set apart from his native-born colleagues. He is not a stranger hereabouts, not out of place among the home-town citizens, but a wayfarer who feels at home in many cities and bears the incidental marks of a distant origin.

In any gathering of intellectuals he is given away by his accent and eccentricity, although I suspect that the latter is often

19

feigned to satisfy the expectation of the Americans. His most distinguishing trait, however, is less noticeable because it shows up among his humdrum daily activities. He performs not only the customary academic work like any of his native colleagues but, in addition, a special role also that he shoulders willy-nilly as an unavoidable burden of his predicament—the role of mediating a foreign culture to America. The culture that he learned in his country of birth might be richer or, as often happens, poorer than the American, but, when transmitted by a creative mind, it is likely to add some enriching elements to our own civilization. In fact, the wayfaring man of learning is different because his career, like an international bridge connecting two countries, offers him a chance to overcome the obstacles of language, parochialism and closed-mindedness, and contribute to the mutual understanding of peoples and the establishment of a common human civilization.

All these are not meant to say that he has two homes. The examples of proverbial sea captains and traveling salesmen notwithstanding, every man has only one home. The extra role that the wandering scholar shoulders means something else: that America with her wealth and the learned wayfarer with his knowledge are engaged in a common enterprise directed toward some distant goal. For this reason the foreign-born scholar deserves the attention of the reader; in the present book he asks for it. The wayfarer (especially if he is of an observing nature) always has something to say about the countries he saw and the country he is observing now; when the mood strikes him, he is eager to settle down and tell his story.

This symposium is a joint venture of a few wayfarers who wish to tell their observations, experiences, opinions or, in general, the problem they represent. They take up many topics but essentially talk about the home and homelessness of people, the geographical limitations of knowledge, and the American attempt to overcome age-old barriers. They talk as learned men and Americans and include themselves in the great and simple self-reference of "we Americans." They talk in a personal manner but their essays, confessions or meditations have a catholic concern. Each of them speaks for himself and presents his own viewpoint. When brought together, they were encouraged, or asked outright, to put aside the professional impersonality of Academe, and they obliged. Hence, they disagree among themselves.

By chance or by design—in this Freudian era one hardly dares to distinguish between the two—the following essays are paired, imperfectly but perhaps argumentatively. In their sequence they seem to follow a dialogue, at times a disputation, by discussing the same topic from different angles and taking different positions. It might be the independence of academic disciplines, the extent of personal involvement, or the variety of beliefs that makes the interlocutors disagree on such a wide range of subjects as the psychological adjustment of the migrant, the political influence of the foreign-born, the administrative system of our education, and the teaching of English in our colleges. It does not really matter. The interlocutors are scholars for whom disagreement is a professional obligation.

Anyhow, the immigration of learned men is not a problem of the order of juvenile delinquency or drug addiction on which we all agree. Mobile scholarship is a sort of problem that people can discuss without any attempt for a general agreement or any demand for urgent social action. It is properly so. Discussion rather than action is the essence of scholarship because discussion helps to generate understanding. In the present venture the participants do not aim for civic resolutions worded for the unanimous approval of the Americanization committees or the organizations of ethnic America. But, in spite of their nonconformism, independence and disagreement, they still stand on a common ground and hold many views in common, first of all, the view of scholarship as a non-national affair, as something that unites, and not divides, mankind. They hold that in contemporary mass societies, where national borders and geographical barriers have become antiquated, the international production of knowledge, the global transmission of ideas, and the even distribution of the same general learning are pressing problems. They hold that America has taken the leadership in solving these problems, in becoming a great producer of knowledge for the use of all nations and a generous provider of homes for the learned men from many places. They view themselves as parts of this venture, engaged in a common enterprise and following some distant goal beyond the usual range of human planning.

In this symposium they offer comments and experiences, assessment of the past and advice for the future progress of the venture.

*   *   *

It is my editorial duty to close on a more personal note and acknowledge the help received in preparing this symposium. I am greatly indebted to David Riesman of Harvard University for his many suggestions and thorough criticism of the manuscript. I am thankful to my old friend Paul Tabori and the editors of the review *Arena* (London) for their encouragement in our venture and their permission to republish four articles that in earlier versions appeared in that review. I owe a special gratitude to a group of medical people at Harvard Medical School—to Robert J. Haggerty, Joel J. Alpert and Margaret C. Heagarty in particular—with whom I could so often and so fruitfully discuss the issues of the service and maintenance of knowledge. Finally, and perhaps in the name of all contributors, I should thank a great many unnamed people—colleagues, scholars, citizens—whose helpfulness, hospitality and companionship have assisted so many wayfarers building a home in America.

J.K.

The Home of the Learned Man

The Company of Seneca

An Essay on the Restlessness of Scholars of All Ages

FOR MY FIRST ENCOUNTER with the immigrant scholar I have to go back in time and recall those years of my youth when the world seemed to be safe and secure, when life and play seemed interminable and inseparable. I spent those pleasant years in the company of thirty-odd boys at the Latin School of Budapest where we applied ourselves to classical studies so diligently that Antiquity became the main concern, nay, the living reality for us. The current topics of soccer games and girls occupied our interest only for the idle minutes of small talk, because the foremost matter on our minds was an issue of the classical world: whether Seneca or Epictetus was the greater philosopher. On this issue we could plunge any time into animated debates which, alas, failed to settle the question. The preference for one of the philosophers was a choice of personal creed; it was beyond reasoning and could not be changed by logical arguments; nothing but graduation put an end to our continual debates.

We were foppish school boys, to be sure, but our scholastic factionalism had a great deal of sincerity and self-consciousness in it. The two philosophers captivated our adolescent fancy because they seemed to represent the human essence. They spoke to us not only through their books but also through their conduct of life, through the romantic turns of their fates and the colorful events of their luck and misfortune, and they seemed to convey to us a message that was the inner reality of our education and the essence of the Latin School.

Seneca, the son of Hispania who spoke Latin with the thick accent of his native province and wrote it with a refinement unsurpassed by other authors, was an eminently successful man in

Rome. He achieved fame and dignity as imperial adviser and statesman, as writer and philosopher; he bathed in opulence and happiness as owner of large estates, as husband adored by a beautiful wife, and as teacher admired by faithful students. Having made good in life, he managed to turn death itself into a heroic triumph. Upon the command of the tyrant Nero, he cut open his veins, and, while his old blood was slowly dripping out, he dictated to his secretaries the last meditations on life and wisdom.

Epictetus came from Greece, the land of wits and dreamers, and reached Rome as a slave. When his master put him to the torture, Epictetus remarked with composure, "You will certainly break my leg." This accordingly happened, and the philosopher added: "Did not I tell you that you would break it?" He was crippled, unattended, and destitute; he taught in Greek and perhaps never mastered the Latin; and his earthly possessions consisted of a bed, a pipkin, and a clay lamp. Yet he taught all who came to listen until Emperor Domitian banished the philosophers from Rome. Then he retired in the provinces and died unnoticed, leaving behind some unpolished books taken down by inept disciples.

In the Latin School of Budapest we became captivated by such vagaries of fate. With the curious sensitivity of adolescent minds we attempted to decipher the message hidden behind the events of life, and we perceived the two philosophers as the archetypes of scholars, as the clearest embodiments of those drives that move all men of learning. Seneca aspired to success, pursued it obdurately and cunningly, and held it in his hands as firmly as it was possible in a murderously competitive society; Epictetus stood for his ideas, doggedly and single-mindedly expounded them to an uninterested world, and did not let pain or humiliation interfere with his lifelong office of teaching. The two of them are timeless symbols because success and stand make the scholar.

Let us not be deceived by educational commonplaces. Knowledge in itself is not enough for a scholar; the idiot savant will never be our hero, and the many-volumed encyclopedia will never be our favorite reading. Any scholarship worthy of admiration must contain the human element; in some mysterious way it must merge knowledge with the deep-seated drives of the personality; it must appear, speak, and act as a natural part of one's personal life. It is the human and subjective use of knowledge that separates the many from the few, because many are those of prodigious memory whose knowledge is great on one or sundry matters, but few are able to combine knowledge, success, and stand into a human unity that arouses posterity's admiration.

Success and stand—are they not elusive words? In a mundane sense, success means the possession of money, power, and fame; the mastery of all goods available to man; the free consumption in one's privately owned land of milk and honey. In a sublimated sense, however, it means the achievement of something immaterial and personal; the mastery of ideas, dreams and illusions; the conquest of people, not by sword, but by word. It means that one's ideas come alive and set out on a life of their own; they become public, are taken up by others, live in the hearts and on the lips of contemporaries and their posterity. The scholar has no intention of imposing himself as a corporeal entity upon others and seeking vulgar popularity. The accessories of mundane success, prestige in the international brotherhood of scholars or status in the chummy community of suburbanites, might incidentally come to him like other chance elements of a professional career; but (and behold the dying Seneca) what he desires as the goal of his achievement is the acceptance of the ideas for which he stands.

Does not everybody have ideas? As the nursery rhyme claims, Peter, the pumpkin eater (who had a wife and could not keep her), conceived some ideas on economical husbandry and proceeded to act upon them. But Epictetus, the other conspicuous failure by all mundane standards, used his ideas for a broader, more penetrating aim: to explain this world of confusing, misty, and self-contradictory phenomena; to create light in the darkness, security amidst anxiety. He had an aim more substantial than Peter of the nursery rhyme, and so have all the scholars who long for creating order in the chaos. But a man can explain the world only in his own terms, for himself and for the satisfaction of his inner restlessness. His exposition—even though it is presented for acceptance by others—is always a part of himself, of his personal essence; it is his pound of flesh and blood that he is ready to defend against the Shylocks. Hence, any creative scholar who once formulates and announces his explanation of the world or of any phenomenon, is prepared to uphold and defend it, stick to it as to a most precious possession, and stand for it as a living symbol. His stand, like probity, is individual and incommensurable. It cannot be measured by yardsticks, and it may be greatest when it amounts to little by the usual standards of success. This is why our youthful debates on the respective merits of Seneca and Epictetus could not be settled. They remained undecided, yet they were not wasted because they led us to a comprehension of the psychological sources of knowledge.

The heroes of youth do not entirely vanish from our memory. They retreat, but they are willing to return, when summoned, in the critical moments of adulthood and discharge the heroic duties of teaching, inspiring, animating. It was no surprise that in such a moment of my life the two philosophers revisited my memory and brought along a new message, fitting my changed conditions. By that time, the Latin School of Budapest had disappeared from my sight, the old masters and schoolmates had dispersed in all directions, and I, taking up a new life in a new country, was riding the academic circuit in America, as one of the many wandering teachers of a continent rich in campuses and inquisitive students. The wanderer, whose home is on any campus or perhaps on none of them, searches for friends and relations, and if he does not find them among the living, he looks around among the dead. So I happened to discover a secret affinity binding me to the paragons of my youth. Seneca and Epictetus appeared to me as the eternal examples of wandering scholars who had left their native provinces, had come to the great campus of imperial Rome, and, together with Paul of Tarsus and many other contemporaries of lesser names, had offered to make their stand and success there.

The showcases of history, arranged for our edification, display the eminent people of all epochs, and in the display, scholarship appears as an eminent but peregrinating profession. In one epoch, the sophists of ancient Greece carried their knowledge from city to city; in the next era, philosophers of all provinces headed toward Rome; then the academic market place of Paris and Bologna attracted professors and students from all Christian countries; later alchemists and humanists wandered from one prince to the other, looking for the stone of wisdom, a rare manuscript, or a generous patron; then modern times came with their wars and revolutions, and each bloody event sent men of knowledge moving.

One may argue that this restlessness of scholars of all ages is just one of those optical illusions that history plays with us. We remember only those men of learning who achieved fame in many cities and in more than one country, and we are apt to forget the sedentary savants and their inconspicuous careers. History is all too often a false mirror, but not in this case. Somehow I think that scholarship and wanderlust are intimately linked by those unfathomable human drives that direct man's career and launch him on an inevitable course of life. Is not search for new knowledge (or any learning for its own sake) an imaginary travel unto an unknown land, which might be a land without geography, an abstract province of ideas, or an eerie road where the scenery is reduced to mathematical formulas? Is the scholar such a bookish homebody that he is unwilling to leave his favorite armchair for a real destination? I would think that imaginary travel and actual travel complement each other. It is natural that after years of spiritual traveling the scholar should bodily take to the road and proceed toward the country of his dreams.

Scholarship and wanderlust meet because the desire for success and the compulsion to take a stand set people on the move. That desire and that compulsion prompt man to relinquish his place of birth where life is familiar, ways are secure, and faces well-known. They induce him to defy the angry oceans of humanity and seek a new home amidst strangers. They make him invest his industry and endurance, pioneer in a wild country, clear the primeval forest, fight the savages, and build a new land for himself.

What is the profit of his investment? The old pioneer trekking westward in his covered wagon searched for God's country, and the old scholar, traveling with his gown and books, looked for the world that is explained and understood, ordered and penetrated, by human reason. When reading their history, we must be impressed by the endlessness of their search. The pioneer cleared a homestead and then moved on; the scholar set up a workshop and soon deserted it; they acted as if they had no desire to end the quest. Life is indeed too short to find what one is looking for, and it is a matter of personal taste what kind of treasure we set out to obtain. In this sense, the scholar is a treasure hunter of adventurous predisposition, more interested in searching than in finding. But he is not a tramp and knows what star he intends to follow. The country that promises chance for success and freedom for stand attracts him. Ancient Rome and modern America are the great examples.

America was founded by migrants and her vast expanses did not allow the migrant to tarry long at the first port. On the horizon of the first settlement, beyond the wilderness, the mountains, and the prairies, she always projected the misty outlines of a distant promise, inspiring the citizens to pull up their stakes and try their luck at some other place. She taught her citizens to enjoy the adventures of physical restlessness and the pleasures of wandering; she bestowed respectability upon wandering, made a national virtue out of it. The Gypsy takes to the road to escape the humdrum toils of work and the respectable monotony of sedentary life; but the puritanical nomad of America—this civilized wanderer constantly on the go, but with law and order deeply impressed upon his conscience—rides his canoe, covered wagon, automobile, or airplane with the expectation that the trip will lead him to his proper place of work. He wanders as a work habit. He takes up his abode wherever his work calls him; he offers home to any stranger who is willing to take up useful work. And in his nomadic civilization, amidst the many kinds of work, scholarship also receives its place.

When Harvard University celebrated the two hundred and fiftieth anniversary of its founding, Mr. Justice Holmes cast a glance upon the venerable history of his Alma Mater and another glance upon the multitude of Irishmen, Poles, and Slovaks who were just crowding into the cities of Massachusetts, and declared: "Civilized men who are nothing else are a little apt to think that they cannot breathe the American atmosphere." The festive orator, an arch-American as he was, did not intend to condemn his fatherland as a country of intellectual barrenness or add fuel to the fire of prejudice smoldering in the cities of Massachusetts. What he was alluding to was an obvious fact for men of his age. There was a gaping chasm between scholarship, as the luxury of long-established upper classes, of Boston Brahmins and Philadelphia Mainliners, and immigration, the desperate rescue action of the poor, downtrodden, and exploited in the backward and badly governed provinces of Europe.

He was right. America attracted the raw manpower of Europe, the surplus population of countries where freedom and food were scarce. She attracted the Joes and Stanleys of Eastern Europe whose paths led to the steel mills of Buffalo or the pushcart business of the Lower East Side. She attracted the men of physical energy who hoped to get ahead with the aid of their muscles, vigor, and sweat. The scholar, this pretentious son of civilized leisure preferred to stay on the other side of the Atlantic. True enough, the three mighty founders of colonial theology—Thomas Hooker, Thomas Shepard, and John Cotton—had come from Emmanuel College in the old Cambridge and helped to establish divinity in the new Cambridge at the Charles. From that time on, the English supply of ministers, teachers, the literal-minded younger sons of the gentry had never dried out; yet, for a quarter of a millennium, the teachers at Harvard constituted an inbred group whose life path ran between the College and a congregation in New England and who abhorred to tread on a strange road.

The trickle of scholarship never ceased. Each convulsion of that fickle continent, Europe, sent a few scholars scurrying across the Atlantic, but these few savants in America were easily lost amidst the multitude of powerful muscles. They went not to the colleges, where the ecclesiastical influence was too strong to suit their tastes, but to the teeming cities of the continent that offered freedom and refinement. Look at Philadelphia as it was about 1800, the glamorous city of Franklin and Jefferson. Here lived mild old Joseph Priestley, the "eighteenth-century Bertrand Russell," who had been attacked by a mob of Tories in England, driven across the Atlantic where he continued to preach, search, and write his vast *History of the Christian Church*. Similar fate brought over Thomas Cooper, once a publicist in old Oxford and now Jefferson's intimate friend, destined to become the first professor of science in the new University of Virginia. In a little stone schoolhouse of the city

Alexander Wilson was teaching; he had been a poor lad from Scotland who, on his first walk in America, had spotted a red-headed woodpecker sitting on a green branch. This delightful sight inspired him to compile his great *Ornithology*. Around the boardinghouses of the city the French émigrés swarmed, among them Constantine Volney, author of the popular *Ruins* on the downfall of absolutism and of a scientific study on the soil and climate of the United States. Next to him one could meet Brillat-Savarin, of the fame of the *Physiologie du Goût*, who took a generous sampling of American food but failed to persuade his hosts to drop their puritanical prejudice against gluttony.

The city is loquacious, inquisitive, and sophisticated; it is the natural habitat of scholars. The foreign-born men of learning gathered in the few cities of the continent where they could live by their wits. Much later, it happened that the colleges of the country ceased to be schools of divinity, admitting secular knowledge and, in the same spirit, teachers from foreign countries. Harvard initiated this movement, and through its open door many distinguished names entered. The Agassiz family came from Switzerland; the father arrived for an exploration but stayed at Cambridge to organize the Lawrence Scientific School; the son turned scholar and entrepreneur and gave away as secret subsidy to learning the fortune he made in copper mining. Hugo Munsterberg, "the great Teuton," came to establish the laboratory of experimental psychology where experiments succeeded, but psychology got somehow lost. George Santayana, a fellow countryman of Seneca, learned his first English words at the age of nine in a Boston kindergarten; when he returned to Spain at the age of twenty, he felt like a foreigner so he settled in Boston where he kept complaining of his captivity among the Puritans. Bernard Berenson arrived from Lithuania and remained cunningly reticent about his early years; but, having passed through Harvard, he somehow emerged as the prince of art history, which is the history of many princes.

"What did you bring?" is the question that people ask of the traveler at his journey's end. One could answer that the scholars brought the refinement of their native countries, the old traditions of learning that lived within the historical settings of Europe. But this would be a flippant and false answer. Out of the names just mentioned, only two received their training in Europe, while the younger Agassiz, Santayana, and Berenson were the academic products of America. To be sure, all of them brought along personal problems that made their quest for success and stand different from that of their native-born colleagues. Somewhere in their careers they developed a special sensitivity, characteristic of those who are in minority; they developed the feeling of being tainted with something that in lack of another appropriate word must be called the vestiges of Europeanism. Yet, in spite of such differences, no great adjustment was necessary for them. They came to live in nineteenth-century America, the not-yet-established, still-flexible America which demanded so little from her immigrant children and was so willing to follow European patterns.

There is something sad in describing one man as American and another as French or Russian or Spanish. By this act we admit our general failure in establishing the one and undivided mankind, the unity of the children of the earth. By this act we admit our weaknesses and limitations, our submission to the tribal idol of modern times, nationalism. We are made Americans, Russians, or Spaniards without our will by the incidental fact of our birth. Nationality is the most painful example of man's dependence on contingencies, his powerlessness against the blind forces of the environment, his insufficiency and inability to form himself according to his ideals. The scholar is, of course, somewhat better than the butcher, the baker, and the candlestick maker because he attempts to overcome the restrictions of nationality, to be an international individualist, and to make his stand and success in global terms. The nineteenth century, furthermore, was the golden epoch of high hopes that men of all nations would become free, reasonable, and united; the scholar was permitted to be an internationalist and, if he had come from another country, was permitted to live by his own law in America.

The nineteenth century was an era of unlimited opportunities, when success came naturally, perhaps even easily, to men in all occupations. The immigrant scholar was moved in his career by the same forces that propelled Pulitzer, Jacob Riis, Carl Schurz, or the captains of industry. He shared with his generation the belief in the entrepreneurial spirit; he trusted himself, relied on personal resources, and looked confidently into the future. He took his stand as he chose. He came to a country which set store by the idea of progress, rejected dogmatic fights, and permitted him to announce whatever philosophy he professed. The aristocratic philosophy of Santayana and Berenson did not evoke opposition in an epoch which was proudly non-aristocratic and often vulgar; and the left-wing political economy of Victor L. Berger and Louis C. Fraina was not silenced with the Palmer raids and the Bridgman convention. What appeared to be a scholarly matter was left unnoticed by the masses and untouched by the officials.

Harvard, the great institution that has carried the burden of academic tradition, stability, and dignity since the beginning of this country, represents only one facet of American scholarship. Another kind of learning has also existed in this country, a homespun learning, fitting the national spirit of restlessness, which has never felt quite at ease amidst the leisurely ways of serene academe, but has preferred to live on the road, visiting the citizens from town to town. America has always been a country of itinerant preachers and scholars who have carried around a self-assertive, aggressive, even folksy scholarship; who have been sometimes sincere and other times sham; but who, in any case, have reached those classes of the country that Harvard left untouched.

The itinerant scholar is a colorful historical character that deserves to be rescued from oblivion. Here is one of them (and he shall be left unnamed because it is no business of mine to separate the truth and untruth about this rather legendary figure) who combined in himself the quackery and the grandeur of the species. He came from Germany as the emissary of a mystical school of philosophy and rode the American lecture circuit around the turn of the century. He believed in his own words and was not afraid of social adventures; he chalked up a memorable success in non-Harvardian America. When, at first, he lectured in German and the audience was set to hear him in English, the lingual confusion did not prohibit his popular acceptance as an authority on the subject. When, later, he arranged evening seminars in philosophy, lecturing in half-lit parlors and serving tea in Russian style with rum, the mixture of tea and philosophy proved to be another success, and the urbane ladies of the audience kept coming back for both.

The present-day respectability of the academic profession (in fact, of any profession) is of recent origin, and not long ago the professional differed but a shade from the carnival man. But in any case, useful work is independent of respectability, and the itinerant scholar served knowledge just as faithfully as the itinerant preacher served God. His service was more than personal. Itinerant scholarship has been one of our national institutions that has come to serve as a popular check on the institutional academe and as a pleasant refuge to the non-conformist man of learning. Stemming from a long-established suspicion against institutional learning, it has worked well to save the academe from rigidity and stuffiness and to keep American scholarship flexible and inventive. It must have been irritating for established scholars to see those outsiders competing for the honors of solid academe, but competitive erudition is one of the great contributions that America made to learning. It prompted our universities to invite guest lecturers from all countries of the globe and all walks of life, issuing invitations, perhaps without much selectivity, but succeeding because of their free and easy manners of welcome. They performed a historical mission by not being selective and inviting those whom the academic officialdom of Europe had rejected. They invited pedants, prigs, pedestrians, erudite fakes, and freewheeling ignoramuses, but they welcomed Freud, Ferenczi and Adler also, and (if I am permitted to mention Canada under the same breath) granted a brief but official stay to Ernest Jones. And although their illustrious visitors left America after a short sojourn, analytic psychology took up a permanent domicile here and reshaped the mentality of the nation more than any idea since Rousseau's time had ever done.

The flow of academic sojourners increased in volume and speed. By 1930 German professors were so regularly visiting our campuses that, when Hitler took over their fatherland, they could easily change a visiting lectureship into a regular professorship. The change, of course, was more than a matter of academic rank and title; it was a product of history, that senseless and wicked history that in the term of one man's life could wipe off the old design of life, politics, scholarship, and happiness. Freud is a historical figure not only as the maker of an epoch, but also as the witness to the decline of Europe. In his middle years, when he came to lecture at Clark University, he had a home in that stable and secure Europe that was the continent of liberal traditions, freedom and progress, wit and erudition; but in his old age, when he came to be a refugee dying in England, he saw around him a sight more painful than cancer itself— Europe in the throes of totalitarian revolt, effacing its noble past.

The totalitarian Moloch swept away the liberal traditions and set up a thought control more vicious than anything devised by Emperor Domitian. It demanded that every citizen accept the cheap ideology of the men of power; it denied the right to say "nay"; it even denied the right to select martyrdom. The spectacular death of Seneca or the dignified withdrawal of Epictetus could not be repeated. The totalitarian Leviathan took control of citizens' fate and proceeded to make yes-men out of the scholars. Few were those who with cunning or luck succeeded in speaking up. Pitirim Sorokin could force Lenin into a debate before leaving Russia on a trip that eventually led him to become one of the founders of American sociology. Salvador de Madariaga (engineer, professor, diplomat, politician, and, perhaps, the last renaissance man produced by the Latin race) gained access to the forum of the international press when totalitarianism subdued his Spain. Einstein, never lost for words when important issues were at stake, always got a hearing because of his unique fame.

But these were the exceptions. The average man was forced to take his stand on a petty issue, as in the case of the German professor whose hour of decision came when the authorities objected to his examination essay: "To what extent may Carlyle be considered a precursor of National Socialism?" Others were forced to recant; an Austrian Nobel Prize winner was induced to deny his conviction and to extol the human greatness of the Fuehrer, a humiliation that did not spare him the necessity of escaping shortly afterwards. And finally, thousands were deprived of speech, action, and freedom, of any sign of human dignity; they were hunted down like beasts because of their race, faith, party affiliation, or success. In face of that totalitarian brutality, how helpless and innocent those sophisticated scholars were. My memory summons up T. L., the friendly sharer of my youthful studies and work, an Epictetus man himself, who, as a young author of fine historical essays and a virgin in mind and body, still expecting life to open up, met his death in a concentration camp.

The hunted and humiliated fled, and their flight was unlike that of the Jews from Egypt, directed by heavenly signs and God-sent leaders. Theirs was a panicky escape, without promising signs in the sky and appointed leaders on the earth; everybody ran in the first direction sighted and slipped into the country which had a back door ajar. But strangely enough, the fugitives beheld before their eyes a land of promise, America. In New York, Chicago, and Los Angeles these were the years of depression—of unemployment, soup-lines, and federal relief agencies with alphabetical names. But those who flee in terror rely on instinct rather than on calculation, and, instinctively, the fugitive mass saw in America not dejection, but hope. Was it not the country of fabulous success where uncles and cousins had made good? Was it not the country with a propensity for attending lectures and studying useful and useless subjects? Was it not the country of itinerant scholars ready to lend an ear to ideas of any origin?

To attract not the raw manpower but the sophisticated intellectual of Europe—this was a new role for America. Back in the nineteenth century the intellectuals who had escaped from Russia, Prussia, and other police states gathered in Paris, London, and the scenic cities of Switzerland. Where else could a European intellectual live? The Russian refugees from the Bolshevik revolution frequented the same cities, and Nabokov states that they abhorred the sprawling, noisy, and vulgar America. But in the 1930's the geography of the world suddenly changed, at least for the refugees; either the world became smaller or their view expanded. Anyway, they discovered America as a country in which one could live. And with this discovery, America came of age. The youthful country of pioneers had turned into a mature land that attracted scholars.

In spite of her inhospitable immigration laws, America was a hospitable country, sympathetic, compassionate, and ready with practical help. What she extended to the hunted and humiliated ones was not the friendliness of her officialdom (is there any country where the officials would be helpful to the homeless and penniless?), but the living traditions of Puritanism and Quakerism, the active principle of charity and admiration for those who take a stand. What she offered was practical helpfulness, organized charity, systematic humanitarianism, and she offered these particularly to those who believed in a creed of their own, who had the courage to oppose and speak up for their conscience. She offered all this as the spontaneous actions of her private citizens, who volunteered help so readily that even the most diligent historian is unable to ennumerate all the acts of charity. Just one of her organized philanthropies, the Emergency Committee in Aid of Displaced Foreign Scholars helped more than 600 men and women; and just one of her professors, Alvin Johnson, established a special University in Exile at the New School for Social Research.

As the refugees came in numbers, popular charity faced the dilemma of how to treat them. They were hungry and needy, but they were not the ordinary poor whom charitable ladies were wont to present with food baskets of ham and turkey. They were intellectuals but could not assert themselves in the respectable manner of our college towns. Who were they, and what treatment should be given to them?

The fine points of the dilemma are best summed up by two literary witnesses. One of them is Randall Jarrell whose picture of the Rosenbaums, that unforgettable couple at the fictional Benton College, reflects the American reverence paid to the foreign-born scholar. "Their kind was a European kind," Mr. Jarrell tells us of the Rosenbaums. "In ungracious moments I felt that their minds were traps in which things came to an already-agreed-upon end; and they must have felt that my mind was so open that things streamed through it without coming to any conclusion at all. And yet—and yet . . . There was a hardness and matter-of-factness about Europeans, sometimes, an accustomed dismissal of what no one could dismiss—no one, surely, ever become accustomed to—that I was troubled by: they brushed life aside as though they themselves were life, and could afford

to do as they chose with it." This is one of those admirable statements of Mr. Jarrell in which clarity and opacity blend to produce what is more than truth—atmosphere. Yet, in spite of all
the atmospheric content, the reader may question whether
America is the land full of Natty Bumppos and Europe is the
fatherland of superiority feelings. On my part, I rather think
that any continent is likely to furnish us with colleagues who
possess that Absolute Superiority that comes from Knowing-
Something-Better-than-Anybody-Else.

Instead of refuting Randall Jarrell, I prefer to call another
witness who under the improbable name of Bravig Imbs turned
out an equally delightful college novel. Here again, among the
colorful figures of an imaginary college, the reader may meet
Nadia Schultz Rosenkrantz, the Russian-born wife of a mathematics professor. She was regularly invited to the respectable
parties of the town on the condition that she would wear her
national costume; and so she did, although she felt uncomfortable with those rattling wooden beads around her neck. Here, I
am afraid, is the crux of the matter. The immigrant scholar was
supposed to be maddeningly superior and, at the same time,
genuinely "folkish," sophisticated and naïve, loyal to his native
country and a civic-minded booster of our social life. To put it
shortly, he was not supposed to be un-American but not entirely
American either.

True enough, all too many of those Rosenbaums and Rosenkrantzes have settled down with no smaller idea than that of
reforming America. It is our good luck that they have never
been able to agree among themselves on the actual content of
those reforms; otherwise, they might have turned America into
a second-rate Europe. Of course, they wanted to reform their
native countries too, although countries in general stubbornly
resist any efforts for reform, let alone reform by people of good
will and reason. In addition, the potentials of an immigrant as
a reformer in America are limited by natural causes. One cannot
live in America for any length of time without feeling the rattling
wooden beads around his neck become uncomfortable. One
cannot live in America without being carried away by her. That
very puritanical spirit that has been so helpful to the persecuted
ones has a strong persuasive power and molds everybody in ac-

cordance with its gentle design. As a result, the Rosenbaums and Rosenkrantzes gladly put down their national costumes when permitted to do so, became Americanized without even noticing it, and gave up their plans for remodeling America.

The refugee from Hitler brought in his intellectual luggage a zest for reforms, a passionate involvement in politics, and a subtle inclination for adjustment. He also brought with him (as an inalienable part of himself that no customs officer could tax or confiscate) his scholarship. His was the aristocratic scholarship of Europe, born in the medieval universities, grown under the tutelage of great masters, and reaching its full maturity about 1930. His was a basically theoretical scholarship, guided by philosophy and history, the two European disciplines *par excellence*, and expressed with the easy rhetorical grace of Seneca— a sound scholarship which, however, could not serve him for long. On this side of the Atlantic he was confronted with American pragmatism, taking its guidance from natural sciences and statistics, expressing itself objectively, impersonally, and often artlessly, and aiming for nothing less than a democratic and popular distribution of knowledge.

Suddenly, the newcomer had to realize that scholarship has two faces and that its Janus character is more confusing than we are ready to admit in the presence of undergraduate students. He was forced to recognize that knowledge is not a closed and rigid system, but the outcome of human conditions, and that as social conditions and personal sentiments change from time to time and from place to place, knowledge must also change. It was a formidable and challenging recognition. The immigrant scholars needed security more than anything else, and now the new country demanded that they should learn to live with Janus-faced knowledge. Many of them refused to give up the notion that their scholarship (and their social system, sentiment, and conviction) were the only correct ones. Others, who perhaps were of more flexible disposition, accepted the basic relativity of human knowledge, adjusted themselves to the new requirements, and absorbed the American form of erudition, without forgetting its European form, which was too deeply impressed upon their minds to be eradicated. Thereafter they blended theory and empiricism, worked for a democratic distribution of knowledge, put learning to practical use, labored in applied sciences, and resorted to statistics in testing theoretical hypotheses. With this approach, they contributed to the reformulation, nay, re-establishment of many a discipline.

A mighty case in point is the atomic bomb. The *Official Report* on the development of the bomb tells us: "At that time [in 1939] American-born nuclear physicists were so unaccustomed to the idea of using their science for military purposes that they hardly realized what needed to be done. Consequently the early efforts both at restricting publication and at getting government support were stimulated largely by a small group of foreign-born physicists centering on L. Szilard and including E. Wigner, E. Teller, V. F. Weisskopf, and E. Fermi." What was the stimulus that the foreign-born had and the native-born lacked? Pure Machiavellianism cannot be a special quality of Europeans or, for that matter, of physicists either. Yet, the decision reached by the small group of foreign-born physicists was so novel, awesome, and fateful that it could not be made without a rigorous examination of one's conscience; and every conscience works in its own ways. The immigrant scholar was not directed by that strange compass of our inner life, the Puritan conscience, which is known to have guided many American-born nuclear physicists. With his open mind he was quick to recognize that at the given moment the country's interest demanded moral pragmatism. He acted accordingly, and history vindicated him.

Whether engaged in martial pursuit or peaceful enterprise, the immigrant scholar contributed his share to that profound change that altered scholarship's place in America and America's place in the world. This was the time when America ceased to be the disciple and became the teacher of nations. Her sons stopped their annual pilgrimage to the European universities to pick up a Ph.D.; in fact, the flow of pilgrims reversed itself, and from now on the sons of all nations came to pursue their scholastic aspirations at the American seats of higher learning. To be sure, the American teachers did not renounce their restlessness, they rather increased the mileage of their travels; but from now on they penetrated the foreign countries as a new kind of globetrotters, as grant-sponsored research teams and exchange professors teaching the aborigines the elements of American-type scholarship.

This was the time when scholarship became a national concern and attracted the organizational genius of America. It ceased to be a private matter, was taken over by public agencies, and was fitted into the total fabric of national affairs, just as any other field of productive labor. This was the time when the old, Washingtonian American reached its end and a new America emerged which changed the dimension of the national affairs already existing and created Big Business, Big Labor, Big Government, and, soon, Big Scholarship. The last, which came into the world as one of the war babies of the 1940's, hired the erudite for important jobs in the service of the war, stimulated a mushrooming growth of research organizations, sent a multitude of veterans to college, and proved before a nation wealthy beyond the possibility of usefully spending its wealth the immediate utility of the scholar's work. The nation was convinced by the proof and decided to employ even larger numbers of scholars for peaceful services in government, business, education, and every possible branch of labor.

As things turned out, the instinctive judgment of the hunted and persecuted ones held good. In spite of depression, unemployment, and alphabetical federal agencies, America offered a propitious environment. Her scholarship expanded to proportions never dreamed of, and the man of learning grew with the opportunities. He was called to found new disciplines, organize graduate schools, award doctorates, and to launch research projects and entire institutes. He was solicited to leave the peaceful campus, move to hectic Washington, turn governmental adviser, administrator, policy maker, public figure. He was entrusted with power over ideas, men, money, and politics, a power second to none of the old Senecas. He happened to live in a creative age, and no other group of scholars ever had better chances.

He was just as fortunate in maintaining his stand. Under the traumatic experience of the depression, America cast away her old fear of burning issues that divide the community; the old Calvinistic insistence upon orthodoxy crumbled. The United States of the 1930's was a much divided country in which the ideological left and right were engaged in pitched battles. Amidst the raging civil war of words, the accented voice of immigrant intellectuals was frequently heard and heeded with attentive reverence. Not that the fugitive from Hitler was an opportunist catering to the whims of ideological sects. But he was a versatile and sophisticated contender in the ideological battles, a professional against the amateurish American, for the *Bierhalles*, coffeehouses, and little reviews of Europe had given him a good schooling in this rhetorical warfare. Whatever principles he professed, he was sure to command attention, find sympathizers, and make converts in his new country. The refugee from Hitler was more likely than not to be a humanist like Thomas Mann, and thousands of Americans listened to him. But at the same time Whittaker Chambers took orders from his Hungarian-born comrades, meeting them secretly in the New York Public Library, and not far away, at Yorkville, in the swastika-dotted meeting halls of the *Bund*, German-born *Gymnasium* professors taught Nazism to excitable young Americans. The morality involved did not make any difference. In each case it was an encounter between a foreign-born teacher of ideology and enthusiastic American disciples.

The group of the 1930's arrived at a felicitous moment; they were present at the right time and place, when and where the chances opened up; and they achieved much in every field of scholarship. Their places were hardly secured in America when, as a quirk of history, another kind of refugee knocked on the doors of our consulates and security offices—the fugitive from Stalin.

Two kinds of political refugees, uprooted within a decade, are bound to share a common fate in personal tragedies, panicky flight, and help received from altruistic America. But history never repeats itself; when it uses an old pattern, it adds some new variations. Hence, the anti-Communist refugee became a new historical type, an added color to the American mosaic. His forerunners of Nazi times had come mainly from the German-Jewish culture which, by the time of Hitler, had found a second home for itself in Manhattan and in the Bronx; but the anti-Communist refugee came from that "twilight zone" of Europe which is hopelessly confusing to the American eye because it is broken up into a jumble of small countries and even smaller cultural units. From the twilight zone a motley crew arrived, speaking many tongues, professing many loyalties, and showing a great diversity of wealth and status. They were united in one point only, their staunch anti-Communism, which saved them from submerging unnoticed into the ethnic sea of America and insured them a prominent place in our great national amalgam.

No immigrant group received a warmer welcome from the usually reserved Americans; this time even the officials of the country turned out to greet the newcomers, welcoming them, often, before the TV cameras. No immigrant group struck a chord nearer to the American heart because no idea had a more rousing appeal to all Americans than anti-Communism.

We Americans like to see the world as a clear-cut picture, as an open field where the forces of Good and Evil fight. We bitterly resent any fact, let alone any theory, that would blur the convincing simplicity of this view. Forever we would like to carry this picture with us and pin-point the Evil in all our political and ideological fights. Alas, the results of such efforts all too often turn out to be embarrassing, for we can never completely agree on whether the witches of Salem, or the old Indian chief King Philip, shot down "like a wearied bull-moose in the deep swamp," or Denmark Vesey and the other Negro revolutionaries were indeed the servants of Satan intent on corrupting our world. But now, in the case of Communism, the recognition of the Evil was clear and unanimous as never before. The whole nation, speaking with one voice, said, "Aye."

Anti-Communism corresponded so perfectly to the prevailing sentiments of the country that it needed no propagandists, publicity agents, or other promoters. The refugee did not create or change it; he depicted and properly exhibited it as an appealing symbol and a valiant fighter of the Evil. The American mind never ceases to search for the lost heroes of our national mythology, for Hiawatha, Leather-Stocking and the other figures of moral rectitude who once fought the Evil with that stubborn single-mindedness that the citizen of the Suburban Civilization is somehow unable to marshal. Now the lost hero reappeared and in his broken English—that was just as expressive as the language of Cooper's heroes—announced his unbroken willingness to fight Communism.

Man has many ways of making good his promise. When the great king captured the House of Israel, some of the refugees sat down by the waters of Babylon and wept, but Joel prophesied of locusts laying waste the land, while Daniel learned the tongue of the Chaldeans and grew up to be an interpreter of secret signs. As it happens, the three biblical ways can be distinguished among the modern fugitives also. The first of them produced a rich foreign-language literature in America; the second turned out as professional anti-Communists, public figures and actors on our political stage; and the third stepped into the mainstream of American scholarship. Once there, the modern Daniel was struck with wonder at the sight of the masses, numbers, sizes, and proportions.

By that time mass scholarship was fully developed, and a scholar could not be lonely any longer. Whatever his field was, he met there thousands of colleagues; whatever his research was, he found other teams working on it; whatever his idea was, he heard it announced by many confreres. He had to step up and join the crowd. He was not asked to found new graduate schools or head research institutes, nor was he asked to sit back, meditate, and create according to his pleasure. But he was asked to take his place among many experts and to work as a specialist with a team. In whatever terms his letter of invitation was worded, he was asked to fit himself into an organization and to subordinate his personal ideas to the common goals of bureaucratic erudition.

As a specialist, success beckoned to him. Big Scholarship could offer rewards of which the imperial patron of Seneca or the Puritan public of John Cotton had never thought—a high standard of living and the cornucopia of goods and services that the daily routine of our automated production system delivers to the door of the suburban citizen. But the immigrant scholar, a specialist on the research team as he was, could not be satisfied with this stolid land of milk and honey. He desired more, and mass scholarship gave that, too. It gave him opportunity to pursue his ideas with financial and mechanical aid never before available to scholars, to publish and distribute the same ideas in copies, languages, and countries never before reached by scholarship. True enough, thousands of colleagues competed with him for the attention of the world, and his voice sounded like a faint whisper in the roaring thunder of mass communication. Yet, there was something formidable and, to some extent, dangerous in the power that the efficient mechanism of Big Scholarship put at the disposal of the man of learning. The erudite specialist, relaxing in his suburban home, with the knowledge of his ideas being irresistibly carried to the masses of the East and of the West, conjures up the image of plenty, power, and self-confidence, in naked contrast to that scholastic self-denial that Epictetus made famous.

Indeed, self-denial detracts from bigness, and the Epictetuses in our midst might embarrass Big Scholarship. Our system of producing knowledge needs the company of Seneca, the eminently successful organization men who are conscious of the social origins of their success and are convinced of the necessity of reasonable conformity. They realize that burning issues which divide the nation could undermine its prosperity, and they honestly endeavor to replace the ideological battles of the previous decades with the pleasant, although demure, conformity of an affluent society. They accept a reasonable conformity which manipulates dissent through an appeal to prudence and decency, and which dislikes the use of force and intimidation. The McCarthy investigations did scare the intellectuals, but these were an isolated episode and not routine practice. The era of Big Scholarship is neither harsh nor dreadful; on the contrary, it is alluring, tempting, pampering. It does not impale the dissenter, but gives affluence to the yes-man.

The scholar as a specialist has not renounced his duty to take a stand, but relegated it to an inconspicuous place, removed it, so to speak, from the front lawn to the back yard. The depth of his soul, his drive for stand and creativity, has not changed, but on a superficial level he has made a compromise with the exigencies. He has accepted his job for what it was set up, a job of solving the practical problems of an organization and not an avocation of standing up as the symbol of an idea. He has accepted his home for what it was designed, a Suburbia built for the easy satisfaction of all human wants and not for an uneasy battleground of neighbors. He has accepted his immigrant fate at its face value, put aside the philosophical wars that he once waged in Europe, and made peace with all neighbors of every faith and ideology.

Look around: the examples of the intellectual compromise are abundant. The former Nazi guard and the former inmate of the concentration camp work now side by side on a military research project; the former comrade and the former anti-Communist refugee ally themselves to ferret out the subversives (and sometimes the non-subversives) on the campus; the present-day *condottiere* hires out his skill in making rocketry and overkill weapons to any political system that is willing to pay the price; and the immigrant scholar speaks up more frequently and with greater self-confidence in the *National Review* than in the *Nation*. The iron rule of self-interest governs behavior in mass scholarship, lets bygones be bygones, and lets everyone watch out for his present goals and future gains.

The anti-Communist immigrant, who is by now settled in our midst, does not signal the end of the eternal restlessness of scholars. Each year brings in a fresh wave of men of learning as America, the great employer of the globe, recruits scholars in five continents to supply skilled manpower for Big Scholarship. Let us hope that this influx will continue in the time to come. As long as America attracts the brainpower of distant continents, her economic and intellectual prosperity will be secure.

The jet planes that nowadays deliver the immigrants land a new generation of wandering scholars at our airfields—the fast-moving and prosperous people of the brain drain. They make up a young and happy generation which has grown up without the political persecutions and assorted social evils of earlier decades, and they leave their countries of birth with no other aim than the search for better opportunities. Present-day America, formed by the miracles and dislocations of prosperity, offers these opportunities, although not on the campuses but in the free professions and learned industries. What she needs now is not the anti-Nazi and general humanist of the 1930's, not the anti-Communist and specialist of the 1940's, but the practitioner and the technician who can apply his erudition to the current demands of a growing economy. The country, a world center of medical science, is short of doctors and has to import one-fifth of its newly licensed physicians from abroad. Its vast complex of learned industries, busily engaged in harnessing electricity, processing computer data, utilizing atomic power and exploring space, needs engineers and physicists so urgently that they are invited to come with supersonic speed.

Those who possess the required knowledge and skills, are recruited in five continents among all nations of the world. If you care to examine the national composition of this brain drain, you cannot escape noticing that it reflects a conspicuous decline of European scholarship. It might very well be that the old seats of learning have ceased to produce erudition, or at any rate the practical knowledge that is now needed, and fall behind in that international competition which is now open to all nations of the globe. Thus, at the same time you have to notice a truly global scholarship in which the sons of China, New Zealand and Africa equally participate.

National origin no longer matters. Upon their arrival in America, the sons of all nations—almost equally and almost without prejudice—are received with glamorous opportunities. Two of the eleven civilian scientists selected as astronauts by the National Aeronautics and Space Administration were freshly Americanized immigrants who walked from the naturalization court straight into the inner military sanctum of the space program and entered careers which will orbit them high above the common man. Their careers may not promise to duplicate the creative course of the epochal scientists—of Einstein, Szilard or Fermi—but they can certainly look forward to a remarkable life-work of public achievements and abundant rewards. Indeed, the people of the brain drain are eminently useful; each of them represents a tangible value, nay, has a price tag attached which arouses the curiosity of the public and the interest of the governments here and abroad. In fact, some of the foreign governments seem to be intent on trading their saleable brains as if they were baseball players or perhaps slaves.

To be sure, the wandering scholars of the jet set depend on the government in many ways. Their livelihood and success are tied to the armament industry and related enterprises, and such ties restrain any urge to dissent. By a curious coincidence, the brain drain has reached America in the 1960's, the articulate decade of civil rights, war on poverty, Vietnam, and nonconformism which saw the intellectuals of the country taking a firm stand and even swaying public opinion. But the newcomers seem to remain uninvolved and seem to avoid those embarrassing occasions that may force them to stand up and make a public confession of faith. It might very well be that our social problems are not theirs. After all, they did not cross the ocean in search of freedom and faith; they only took a short trip of convenience. Their journey is so short and easy that they can live coming and going between two countries. My suburban neighbor, the high-priced specialist in an abstruse field of electronics, returns every summer to his native land, explaining his peregrination unpretentiously with "One can work only in America, but one can live only in the old country."

It might be too much to ask such an international commuter to take his stand on civil rights and poverty programs; nobody asked Seneca to speak up when Nero fiddled and tyrannized Rome. Yet, there is a hope for the present-day company of Seneca, the hope of time and patience. As the years pass and their careers progress, they will learn more about the varieties of American life. In addition, they may recognize that the difference between the scholar and the technician is not in the extent of erudition or success but in stand.

And so it happens that scholars from five continents meet in this modern Rome of ours, the greatest Rome of history, that with its sprawling campuses and skyscraping offices extends from Massachusetts Bay to San Francisco Bay. There has not been any bigger and richer Rome yet, no place that would have invited more learned men. Seeing their numbers, let us not lament the absence of Epictetus from the crowd. After all, the company of Seneca is certainly with us, an active, eager, and helpful company that works on the solution of many useful problems and promises to accomplish much more. This company, a colorful group, wearing the emblematic signs of accent and eccentricity as permanent badges that can never be cast off, stands out conspicuously against the native-born majority of the academic profession. But signs are deceptive and emblems are figments. The scholars of our Rome cannot be divided into two camps by their places of birth; they think the same way and work together; they are the best symbols of mankind undivided. And the immigrant scholar, whatever his name, accent, or eccentricity may be, is the strongest promise the human race has ever had that our ancient dream may come true, that a united mankind somehow will be established—a mankind that puts aside tribal warfare and linguistic barriers and stands united in work, scholarship, and, perhaps, even wisdom.

On the Americanization
of Martin Grotjahn

ON SEPTEMBER 24, 1936, I arrived in America with my wife and infant son. Through my glasses I looked at the Statue of Liberty and thought: "At least I have seen her—even if I never get there." I was gripped by a paralyzing fear that in the last minute the German *Bruder* would stop me and with some trick would keep me from going ashore. As a physician, psychiatrist, and psychoanalyst, I had become a rarity in Berlin; the Nazis could have claimed me as an essential. I also could have been considered a security risk since I had worked at the Berlin University and witnessed the events from 1933 to 1936.

Arriving in New York I had $2.50 in my pocket and felt tempted to throw it into the water. I wanted to start all over again, unburdened by anything. The first taxi driver, however, relieved me of this symbolic burden and for a moment gave me the taste of being totally free of my past. Then anxiety flooded me. It was not the old persecutory anxiety of being caught or being annihilated as a free man; it was the new anxiety of having lost my identity.

I felt a kind of kinship with Ahasuerus. I had to accept a new world in which only change itself seemed to be constant; at the same time I had to keep some parts of the past which would support me as a physician, a psychoanalytic scholar and a teacher. What was needed was to be invented and developed— an open-end living, supported by the shared mutual identity of marriage; I felt lucky with my young family centering around a baby who had been born almost in the new country.

Life after immigration repeats the experiences of infancy with its helplessness and of adolescence with its uprootedness. To go through both again is a painful but strengthening experience like a tough initiation rite in which the mother's child is virtually killed and the man is born. To many people, the idea of immigration seemed worse than death, and they actually were killed because they hesitated and missed the last boat.

Passing through New York I was shocked that people really spoke English and nothing else. Although they treated me indulgently as one would treat a precocious child, I could not understand the language of the adults. The work of the analyst depends on communication, and my sudden inability to communicate was as much of a castration experience as any adult can have. It prompted a rethinking in which the matter of shifting languages and changing locations led to a re-examination of my entire analytic orientation and my new identity.

One day I visited A. A. Brill, the American friend and translator of Sigmund Freud, in his office overlooking Central Park. For educational reasons Brill spoke English and never suspected the full extent of my ignorance. He spoke of Freud's visit to America when the two of them had walked in Central Park, and Freud, persisting for 46 years in the same apartment of Vienna, had pointed at the windows of Brill's office and said, "Never move." At that time one did what the professor said, and Brill never moved. I continued to move and never really settled in this world of reality.

The experience of immigration contrasts man's basic hope for recognition with his fear of failure. To this challenge so many scholars have reacted well, and the group of European analytic scholars furnish a case in point. The alienated man in modern America welcomed the alien from Europe in whom he saw an expert in the art of dealing with the problems of existence. This welcome has been a great help.

In Berlin I had been the son of a famous father. In the Middle West, where I moved at the beginning of my American life, I was myself. I cannot claim that the events of the first year resulted in the emergence of a new identity, but they did amount to the required initiation rite during which a part of me died and a new part emerged. The Middle West offered an environment where the retreat into an immigrant enclave was impossible. This helped me to avoid a defensive dogmatism and maintain a spirit of open-mindedness which would not have been possible in one of the great psychoanalytic centers of the east coast.

For a while I remained a curious observer. From behind the couch I watched the American person and the American scene— or perhaps watched myself on the screen of these transitory images. When compared to so many American psychiatrists who started in training just then, I was a little "ahead in the game." I witnessed the rapid growth of psychoanalysis in the United States and felt that I had to show what I could do. Soon, however, I came to realize that my professional capacity was taken for granted; the American colleagues were not questioning my qualifications but were eager to prove their own skills.

I had moved from the psychoanalytic coffeehouses of Europe to the big American institutes of psychoanalysis. For most Europeans psychoanalysis was research-directed; for the Americans it was therapy-directed or patient-directed. This difference caused fateful confusions; it led many immigrant analytic scholars to become dogmatic Freudians who taught the canon but not always the spirit of psychoanalysis. For them, psychoanalysis symbolized the spirit of the old country that had to be transplanted into the fruitful soil of a new country. For them, analytic training became an indoctrination instead of a learning experience. Their kind of analysts formed a bodyguard which kept therapeutic psychoanalytic technique almost unchanged over the last sixty years, a period of so much change and progress in other fields.

Luckily, I could keep my mind open and could combine the European attitude of skeptical investigation with the American attitude of always hopefully looking for new and better tools in therapy. I still think that psychoanalysis is a great instrument of clinical observation and the best method for the study of human behavior and unconscious motivation; but after all these years of clinical experience, I am skeptical about analysis as the last word in psychotherapy.

So the difference between a pioneer and a dilettante became clear to me. My new friends in America lived like pioneers in a psychiatric community where the question was what to do before the analyst would arrive. No one thought he had something better to offer; no one thought he had found something more advanced or more efficient; no one thought he had corrections or improvements to offer; no one was especially resistive or especially rebellious. Everybody tried anxiously to help the best way he knew. It was like in olden times. When there was no carpenter in the pioneer town and houses had to be built, everyone did his best; later when a carpenter came, his workmanship was put to use together with the cruder skills of the pioneer.

I knew of Freud's antagonism toward America and remembered that he excused America's discovery only by the fact that it had led to the introduction of tobacco to Europe. To restore the honor of my new home, I hastened to write him what amounted to a European's "Declaration of Dependence" on America. In this missive I affirmed my faith in the spirit of psychoanalytic pioneering. I tried to show the difference between American and European attitudes, between the pioneer and the dilettante, between early and later times of psychoanalytic history, between old disciples loyal to the tradition and new disciples committed to progress and experimentation. As was Freud's habit, he answered by return mail. He was happy to hear what I had to say and wished me well. But I guess I did not convince him.

After a move to Chicago (where Franz Alexander had established the Chicago Institute for Psychoanalysis according to the design of the Institute of Berlin) I felt more at home. I learned from Franz Alexander the art and logic of psychodynamic reasoning which was his great contribution to psychoanalysis in America. At first it struck me as just another application of psychoanalysis to the quick understanding of people, but soon it became my ambition to apply psychodynamic reconstruction to the American dream of patient-directed therapy. I reasoned that a method which had worked well in understanding psychosomatic diseases could perhaps be used in analytic psychotherapy also. This technique, like many other innovations of Franz Alexander and his team, greatly helped American psychiatry to outdistance the old world in such fields as group and family therapy, and treatment of psychosis. The history of this circle shows an extremely productive relationship between immigrant scholars and native therapists which deeply influenced American culture.*

With the analytic reorientation seemingly accomplished, it seemed natural that I should write and talk about my adventures in the vast field of psychoanalysis. I became an enthusiastic teacher trying to show the students the great wealth of knowledge enclosed in psychoanalysis and the great joys of discovering the truth about oneself with the aid of analysis.

The matter of personal identity was more difficult to solve. Slowly I discovered the truth that in the new world I would have to proceed in personal isolation. The Americans saw a German in me and the Germans an American. My Jewish friends never completely forgave my Prussian background; I had the impression that they would have respected me more had I done what Freud suggested to the non-Jewish analysts in Germany: to fight the German brethren on the home front. My professional place was just as ambiguous. The psychiatrists thought of me as an analyst and the orthodox psychoanalysts classified me as an innovator; the colleagues in experimental science saw a clinician in me and I regarded myself as a clinical observer. There is an old saying about the truly independent man being loved by no one. But are we loved only for belonging to this or that group?

By all means, I wanted to belong to a group and, as soon as it was possible, applied for American citizenship. But the question of whether I was really adjusted or not lost its importance on the day when the Japanese attacked Pearl Harbor. Five days before my citizenship application was scheduled for final action, war was declared; instead of naturalization I had to register as an "enemy alien."

* The best evaluation of the immigrants' influence on American psychoanalysis was written by John A. P. Millet, "Psychoanalysis in the United States" in *Psychoanalytic Pioneers*, ed. Franz Alexander, Samuel Eisenstein and Martin Grotjahn (New York: Basic Books, 1964). In the same book, an essay may be found on Franz Alexander by Martin Grotjahn. There are many other biographies of immigrant analysts in America, namely, Otto Rank, Paul Federn, Edward Nitschmann, Hanna Sachs, Sandor Rado, Theodore Reik, Geza Roheim, Helene and Felix Deutsch, Wilhelm Reich, Ernst Simmel, Sigfried Bernfeld, Paul Schilder, Heinz Hartmann, Otto Fenichel, and Ernest Kris. This essay further refers to books by Martin Grotjahn entitled, *Beyond Laughter* (New York: McGraw-Hill, 1957) and *Psychoanalysis and the Family Neurosis* (New York: W. W. Norton, 1960).

Once more the identity of the psychoanalyst had to be changed. The teacher had to retire for the duration of the war. I gave up my behind-the-couch observation post of the American scene and crossed the troubled waters of the Ohio River to take up work in a newly opened military psychiatric hospital in Kentucky. There a military psychiatrist emerged with surprising ease. No one bothered to tell me anything about army manners and matters, and I became an American officer by virtue of the uniform, speaking an accented English but, at any rate, not clicking his heels.

Back in Germany it had been impossible for me to put on any German uniform even when it had been a matter of life and death. But now the military world offered me a new screen upon which I could transfer my inner world with less conflict. Four years of work as an army psychiatrist made me feel that I earned my right to be accepted by this country. No amount of research or teaching would have given me that freedom from guilt which I achieved in this way; although during the years of war my case was complicated by a brother who was an officer in the German Army and a mother who watched her Cain and Abel fighting.

I joined the post-war migration to California not with the aim of getting rich quickly or staking out my claim in the psycho-analytic boom, not because I wanted to be with the happy people on the merry-go-round or to bask on the beach. Rather I thought that I was through with trying to adjust to a collective team, institution, or organization, and the time had come to start out on the road and see another part of America. We moved like Bohemians having no property except what we could carry in our car. People took this as a demonstration of our disbelief in their set of values; they were right. They gave up their attempts to make us conform; they let us live the way we wanted to live.

Soon I learned that adjustment to the atmosphere of California was not easy either, and finally I accepted the fate of a man firmly rooted in a cloud. For many years I worked mainly as a training analyst and this brought new and fascinating involvements. When a student-patient finished his clinical analysis with me, he did not vanish from the scene like any other patient. He would stand before me as a document of work, done and left undone, visible to all, more or less. His presence was the acid test for a man's belief in his professional efficiency.

Before I could settle into the state of being unsettled, an old problem faced me and demanded new solution. After my first visit back to Germany I felt guilty for having escaped and survived the agony and seeming death of my native country. I felt guilty for being alive, for living in beauty and health, for continuing the undisturbed search for insight. With this problem I asked in vain for help from colleagues, friends, students. In my need to atone for an unconscious guilt, I enraged them by waving the red cloth in their faces so that they would charge at me.

To deal with the return of the repressed is a task that the maturing immigrant cannot avoid. The retrospective attitude of the later years of life revives the love for the old country's tradition, and this repressed love asks for a special understanding of the unconscious. Its solution lies in working through an inner harmony which, then, promises the achievement of what I should call symbolic integration. Living in my unsettled state of California, I think symbolic integration contains the answers to the problems of human existence in the future.

Modern man can no longer live naively but by rational thinking and insight into his unconscious. Rational thinking, when unaided, leads to alienation; and insight, when alone, closes his eyes before the cruel reality around him. What he needs is an integration of all levels of understanding.

Psychoanalysis does not necessarily result in a personal adjustment to the misery and silent despair of everyday life. It does not necessarily bring us the gift of happiness, but it does bring us nearer to an integration of the unconscious into our lives. In my case it has been a personal help in combining the old country's inner-directedness with the new country's future-directedness. In case of America it promises a far more general contribution, and California is the example to prove my point.

In this hospitable state of unsettlement on the Pacific I have never felt as if I were the only migrant. California has impressed me as a gigantic modern harbor where day and night millions of travelers arrive and depart, where all citizens are on the move to emigrate, having as their destination the imaginary Californian future of an eternal sunny Paradise without anxiety and even

ultimate death. But, like children at the end of the vacation, my
fellow migrants begin to sense that no one can travel into the
future without the pain and conflict which naturally accompany
growth and maturation. This is why they come running to the
wise men sitting in silence behind their couches whose figures
symbolize the knowledge of the past and the hope for a happy
future.

All these would mean that my place is here, fixed as definitely
as it can be for any man. My place is the end stop of migration
and Americanization, but my whole peregrination has been just
a part of a larger movement in which the analysts in foreign
countries have been invited to come and contribute to the great
transition of America. We have come, bringing along the analytic
skills we had to serve as personal help to us and general help to
others. In our lives after immigration we might have repeated
the frightening experiences of infancy and adolescence, but, in
the final outcome, we have been given the reward of preserving
the identity of the analyst and the insightful orientation of our
trade.

FRANZ ADLER

The Marginal Man on the Faculty

THE MARGINAL MAN, as the sociologists describe a type common among us, "is in contact with two cultures, participating in parts of each of them, but belonging fully to neither." He is moving away from one social background and working toward his acceptance in a new environment. In this process he either is cut, or cuts himself, loose from his original moorings. At the same time, he is likely to meet resistances to his full integration into the new life. Characteristically, these resistances not only come from the outside, but some, and perhaps the most serious ones, originate within himself.

The migrant from one country to another is a marginal man, but he is not the only one. He who moves from one social class to another, who changes religion, job or school, who grows from one age group into another, who leaves one family to find another, and many others become marginal and remain so for a longer or shorter period of time, even forever. In fact, the world is full of marginal men—there are no others. If this were not the case, all of us would be exact copies of each other, devoid of any glimmer even of individuality, stamped out by the same die; everyone would be a perfectly average man of his social set.

The migrant between two countries is very likely to be marginal in nationality and in other matters as well. The migrant scholar moves not only from one country, language, and culture to another, but also, if he is lucky, from one institution of learning to another. His status in private life may also change, and the impact of a marriage upon his scholarly career should not be underestimated. He may find his accustomed religion or irreligion a drawback to social advancement, may leave it and join another. He may lose old friends and make new ones. And in any case, he grows older. All this may be hard or easy on him depending on such circumstances as the degree to which he has internalized the ways of his earlier environment, the extent of the pressures put on him by the new one, his personal flexibility or inflexibility, his ability or willingness to return home, and numerous other factors.

Let us consider first some of the pressures of the new environment. In almost every case, the migrant scholar must learn to express himself in a new language. His success in managing that new language will depend on the age at which he first comes in contact with it, on the inherent difficulties of the language, on its similarity to his own, on his previous experiences with learning languages, etc. But the attitudes of different countries toward foreign speakers differ widely. Frenchmen consider anybody a barbarian who fails to speak flawless French. In England language patterns of the lower class turn out to be embarrassing whenever upper-class patterns are expected. In Germany western and northern European accents are acceptable, while eastern European accents pose insurmountable obstacles to any advancement.

In the United States, on the other hand, accents (perhaps with the only exception of that of the southern Negro) are quite forgivable. Most Americans, being uncertain themselves concerning the correct spelling and pronunciation of many words, are reluctant to be overly critical of other peoples' mistakes. Thus, many foreigners whose utterances are understood only with effort and difficulty, can be found holding forth in academic classrooms. Only rarely will they be found, however, as deans or presidents of universities and hardly more frequently as department heads or other lower administrative officials. This fact, however, leads us to another kind of pressure of the new environment.

Anybody holding office in an organization must fulfill its formal requirements. The scholar, like any other jobholder, must put in certain hours and do the work for which he is paid. He must obey directives issuing from authoritative sources and give directives to specified classes of recipients. While these arrangements may differ considerably from those to which he was accustomed, and while he may chafe under them and resent them, he can easily find out what they are and decide whether their unpleasantness is outweighed by the intellectual and material satisfactions of his employment. European scholars in the United States often miss the broad freedom of European academic positions, but, knowing the rules as they exist here, they have no difficulty in submitting to them. Frequently they find outlets for their dissatisfaction with the formal system by joining the American Association of University Professors or other similarly ineffective action groups, and there they propagate highly idealized versions of the academic systems of their home countries before audiences who consider such arrangements purely utopian and unworkable.

In the formal systems to which the foreign scholar has chosen to subordinate himself, difficulties arise from features which nobody has explained to him because nobody is aware of them. A German scholar, for example, is used to giving and receiving orders in the linguistic structure and the vocal sound of commands. American orders, almost anywhere outside the armed forces and sometimes even within them, are given in the voice of suggestion. One German professor whose dean had told him repeatedly during the year in a very cordial tone of voice, "Now, if I were you, I would not do this, but would do that," was very much surprised when his contract was not renewed at the end of the year. He felt that he had been informed of what the dean would choose to do in a professor's position and had not the slightest suspicion that he had been given orders. At the same time he antagonized students and secretaries by telling in a tone of military command what he wanted them to do.

Among formal elements most difficult to grasp for foreigners are the ways of academic democracy. The ancient universities of the Old World are truly self-administering establishments whose high degree of independence from any outside influence is strongly supported by the general population. American colleges and universities, on the other hand, are run by boards generally consisting of non-academicians, who are appointed either by political officeholders or by private providers of funds, and who, in turn, appoint the school's chief administrators. The administrators are responsible to these boards rather than to the faculties. The faculties or their elected representatives are at best advisory rather than decision-making bodies; their opinions may be disregarded at any time at the discretion of the non-faculty administrators. The foreigner, however, tends to mistake these trappings of faculty democracy for the real thing. Instead of "playing the game" according to the rules, he may become very much upset debating matters which are, after all, being decided elsewhere.

Administrators do like to maintain the appearance of faculty consent for their actions. Thus they try to construct majorities by consultations with faculty members before anything comes to a vote. The naive newcomer who harangues his colleagues with impassioned speeches notices too late that all has been arranged beforehand and that he is merely holding up the proceedings. He is outraged. What he fails to realize is that it is exactly in the private discussions which he condemns as pure manipulations that some effective faculty influence upon the decision process is exercised.

The formal academic way of life is interwoven with an informal one. Non-business contacts with the persons involved and their spouses occur in many situations. The foreigner who comes from an environment in which titles and ranks were greatly emphasized and never omitted in social intercourse may feel charmed and elated when the president or the dean pats him on the shoulder, calls him Joe, and, in return, expects to be called Al or Tom. He easily forgets that the equality this first-name address seems to symbolize applies only to certain non-business contacts and to a limited extent even in these. He courts disaster if he ever forgets that Al or Tom may still fire him if he oversteps the boundary which is obvious to them and to his native colleagues but invisible to him. Small wonder that only a scholar wise to the ways of this academic world, both formal and informal, will ever qualify for an administrative position in it. By the time he has obtained this wisdom he is likely to have offended more influential people than all his wisdom will ever manage to reconcile.

Environment accounts for only one part of the syndrome of marginality, the other part is connected with the individual himself.

The subtle and not-so-subtle influences of a person's family conditions upon his professional life are numerous and involved. The scholar who arrived in his new homeland with wife, children, or parents is likely to find it more difficult to adopt the patterns expected from him in America than the other who founded a family in the new country. The former may use the imported family as a miniature edition of his old accustomed environment in which he finds shelter after the hardships of life among strangers; the latter may find a native spouse who introduces a conflict of cultures into his family while at the same time eases his adjustment to the outside world. Then again, family members who arrived together may become integrated with the new life at different speeds and to different degrees, and each may resent the other's deviance from his own pattern. Parent-child conflicts and husband-wife tensions become aggravated as they pass from the purely personal into cultural dimensions.

Outside of his family, every man needs to find his place within the complex matrix of the total society, and the need is particularly pressing for the migrant. For the sake of his self-esteem he needs a reference group, that is, a group of people whose judgment matters to him much. Yet, our scholar faces a dilemma even here. If he tries to apply the standards of professional activity valid in his country of origin, he may conflict with the standards of his new homeland or vice versa. The European who, following the patterns of his old confreres, lives in theoretical abstractions may find that his more practically oriented American colleagues fail to see any point in his activities. In rare cases his interest in his old reference group may make him an effective missionary among members of his new one. With success, he may find himself able to change reference groups, accepting the new one as the more important, without really changing his actual predilections. This is what happened during the second World War and thereafter in the United States when foreign-born theoretical physicists and mathematicians working on nuclear weapon developments convinced American scientists of the ultimately practical value of high-level theories.

Strangely enough, a similar choice of reference group, that is, an acceptance of the Old World members of the profession as the ones that really count, may produce exactly the opposite effect. One social scientist explained his development in the United States in the following words: "Back home I never dared to speak out or write because I felt I never could measure up to the demands of the profession. But those critics and judges are far away. The people here do not count; they are not any better than I am. Here I say what I darn well please and feel good about it." Such a liberation from the pressure of a group which is still defined as the only one that really matters has permitted this particular scholar to be quite successful in America. Usually, however, the inferiority feelings which this man experienced with regard to his country of origin are gradually extended to the new country, and this is particularly the case when painful experiences teach that what may have insured success in the past is likely to lead to failure in the future.

In other cases the feeling of liberation, usually a helpful aid to creative activity, may turn into a feeling of utter normlessness, in which the absolute lack of guidelines and limits frightens a person to the point where he is stifled in his creative efforts and may fall prey to neuroses or psychoses. The same may occur when a scholar is torn between his adherence to conflicting reference group ideals, when he is unable to combine the roles that he feels the two groups expect from him and fails to elaborate an integrated image of himself in which he can function effectively.

Some immigrants in all stations of life maintain their personalities undisturbed by withdrawing from the general population and living in a ghetto that preserves the major aspects of the home environment and shuts out all that is foreign. There also are academic ghettos of this kind, and foreign language departments easily lend themselves to such formations. At times a whole school appears whose faculty consists almost entirely of migrants from one country. The result is a cultural enclave, a strangely esoteric ivory tower, quite out of touch with the life that goes on around it.

So far, mainly the dangers and pitfalls of being a marginal man have been stressed. But, as a matter of fact, this position also has its benefits. These rest primarily in the chance that some information or technique may have been accessible to the scholars of one country but not to those of another. When this knowledge suddenly becomes needed and desired, the migrant scholar has a great advantage that must be attributed not only to his personal qualities but also to his luck. So it happened in the case of the atomic scientists in America and, as a reversed situation, in the case of social scientists in Germany. Those immigrant scholars who acquired the know-how of American research technique during the Hitler era and then carried it back to their home country—being there by then almost as marginal as they had been in the United States a few years earlier—found a demand for this knowledge and, in turn, found it relatively easy to become personally reintegrated in the country of their birth.

Indeed, scientists gain a particular advantage from a marginal position. The way a man sees the world is largely conditioned by the speech and action patterns among which he grows up. Thus, what the culture refuses to see, he cannot see; what the culture magnifies, looms large in his sight; and this manner of perception is continuously reinforced as long as his social and cultural environment remains the same.

If he leaves one country and settles in another, there comes a period when the reinforcements of his old perceptive processes have ceased and the pressures of his new environment have not yet succeeded in giving him their own kind of blind spots and distortions. At this point of his personal development he is predisposed to objectivity, to seeing things as they really are; now he has a special chance to make a unique contribution to sciences. By all means only a few of the marginal men reach this freedom of the mind, perhaps only the strong ones who can bear to be free and do not need protection from freedom in a ghetto or a neurosis. Nevertheless, the freedom of the mind that the marginal man enjoys is an invaluable asset; it is the grace saving him from futility.

Let us recall that being marginal is not an exclusive attribute of migrants, let alone scholars. All of us are potentially marginal as we move through life. This is more so than ever before because our society is becoming more mobile and marginality is becoming more general. Thus, it is not vain to hope that, together with this change, the freedom of the mind will also increase and will furnish us with more objective, more reliable knowledge about the social world than the traditional views have done. This knowledge of free minds may help us to establish a more satisfactory social arrangement than those based upon any of the innumerable bankrupt traditions of mankind.

JOHN MOGEY

Assimilation to the
Administrative System

IN THIS ESSAY, we—and the meaning of this pronoun will presently be explained—give a personal description of how the academic organization appeared to a British academic who came to take over the chairmanship of a department. British universities, whether old foundations like Oxford, Cambridge, or St. Andrews, or new civic universities like Belfast, Liverpool, or Manchester, run like a team with the chairman in each department being both liaison man on the team and the sole power in the department. The only full-time administrators are staff men appointed by this academic team to handle routine jobs. Whereas in America. . . .

Anecdotal material recalled after a lapse of five or ten years is notoriously unreliable stuff for a social scientist to use as the raw material for a statement. On this occasion I want to write about personal experiences and so have no other possible source of data. However, as I write, I propose to do two things. First, I want to involve my wife who shared these events and sharpened my perception of them. So instead of *I*, first person singular, I will write most of the time as *we*, first person plural. Second, all episodes written down exactly as they occurred would be as long as a Southern novel, even if total recall were possible. So selection is inevitable, too. I bow to this and think it only proper to say that as *we* write about ourselves in social encounters with other individual personalities we intend to avoid the risks both of offending good friends and of libel by selecting sections of episodes to give emphasis to points we feel are crucial. Having adopted such a policy, we cannot mention names, since in the same sequence one role may have been played by several personalities.

Apprenticeship

When we handed our immigrant papers to the official at New York on a dull warm January evening in 1960, we did not feel strangers to the U.S.A., having spent over a year here on a fellowship. That year introduced us to academic worlds of Chicago, Colorado, and New York. With briefer forays to Boston, to Ohio, to Toronto, and to Washington, D.C., we imagined we knew something of the variety of American academe. We had made friends; we had been welcomed as newcomers. In one place, I had been free to labor on a research project, had perfected my vocabulary in the language of variables, variances, and values, and had learned to control the motions of a counter-sorter machine. In another, I was a free lecturer. Most of all, however, I was a colleague accepted as an equal participant in seminar and conference, advised to write up certain points of view and to forget about others, encouraged intellectually, stimulated by the intense interpersonal relations in the campus at Chicago, exhilarated by the scope and status of the subject I had chosen, sociology. I felt for the first time the acceptance of an adopted son.

In New York we found a more relaxed tempo but curiously felt that a more intense life was being experienced outside of the interactions we were in than inside them. This impression built up slowly and uncertainly. We never could be really sure of it. Either less was going on intellectually than in the Chicago community—but the facts of output and publication did not support this hypothesis—or we had a more peripheral place in the scheme of things; but again, it was hard to find evidence to justify this.

Seminars for a visiting fellow were as exciting as in the Midwest and yet less dramatic. It was as if the participants were so professional they could admire themselves giving a good presentation at the same moment as they were giving it. In the West, guarding and thrusting, give and take, also went on at the conference center; only after the performance did satisfaction with the presentation of self and others become apparent.

It may be that the ecology of New York made for the differences in academic behavior. In the Midwest most people lived near at hand, so office, library, seminar, and evening party could encompass in a close network the same individuals. New York had the same events, but the other network relations between those present were open rather than closed. Consequently, our memory of Chicago was a warm primary-family-center sort; the total warmth of relations in New York was not less but each strand in the network was independent of all others.

Both New York and Chicago as we met them were full of the most literate and articulate types in all of our experience. Not even Trinity College, Dublin, had more vivid and arresting conversationalists. No one, it is true, outdid the Junior Dean there, who to convey the excitement of the West African bar on his promotion, did a dance on the table. But conversation was a joy. So long as we stayed with academics, our values and predispositions were shared by the group.

The point of all this is that as a visitor, doors were open; participation was welcome; friends were warm; feelings were shown in both Western and Eastern universities that have never been seen since. When we tried to recapture this euphoria with these friends visiting Oxford, we were convinced it was the formal English atmosphere that was the only inhibitant.

Returning now as a jobholder to the same academic milieu, I was met by surprise, "But why a Southern university?" and by warning, "Why did you not ask my advice before you took the job?" Individual sociologists sought us out, looked long and wonderingly at us as specimens, bade us welcome as immigrants but were astonished that we had chosen to settle in the southern part of the country. In the following we shall try to separate what was academic in our experiences from what was Southern. The only way we can legitimately do this is by comparisons between like events. Summers were spent at a Western university, and some comparable episodes there help us to make the separation. Southernness as an ethnic characteristic, however, was so pervasive that the distinction is always tentative.

Now is the moment to give our impressions of the different nuances we noticed as between being a visitor and an immigrant. While I was a fellow, the usual oblique warnings were passed to us about the quirks of this or that academic; most went unnoticed for a few months but gradually my wife and I learned to interpret the clues. Not being in the system, even when we recognized cues and understood what was intended, our role was primarily that of the observer. Using the cues, we could merely see a little more of what was going on; we could not participate in it. These perceptions might be called the affective context of interactions, composed of emphases and gestures which qualified what was actually being said. Once or twice, both in Chicago and in New York, attempts were made to involve us on one side or the other of a departmental skirmish, but we did not feel we knew enough of the rules to join in the game. So we could be *in* the group but not *of* it wherever we were, and by the same token, we could hear the "asides" or "stage whispers" which the participants on both sides wanted to be shared with friends only. Being a fellow gave us the status of "visiting friend" to all. As a jobholder, the whole social situation changed. We had to join and declare ourselves as for this, or against that; without this commitment we perceived we would be outsiders or isolates. There were a sizable number of such loners on our Southern campus. One "Southern" liberal was to warn us, however, "the secret is to be concerned without being committed."

Thanks to a series of unplanned encounters in England and at various international meetings, I had the chance to return to the U.S. as chairman of a department, not just as a scholar. This placed me as part of the administrative team in the university system. It was a challenge that I felt I could meet, given some co-operation and good will. We did not rush into the opening; correspondence, promises of good will and co-operation had been exchanged for almost two years. The president had visited with us in Oxford and through his Rhodes Scholar network collected collateral information on my standing and performance there. We had, in turn, sought out all we could find who had ever been in or near "Southern University." "It's a great place" they said, "do come." "We need you as immigrants for the good of this country." So we came back as jobholders.

This immediately changed our image in the eyes of former acquaintances. We had joined their social network and had to be considered as professional colleagues. In this relationship, as is well known, friendship and reputation rarely march hand in hand. More than this, I had joined a department as head. In

spite of all the questions we could ask, it was difficult to discover if I joined the university more as an administration man
or as a department man. More than likely no one knew; the
role could be played either way. The acting chairman wrote in
welcome terms, not fulsome but warm, and openly discussed all
issues and questions that I raised.

Because I had been an undergraduate in a university where
one stream used the Scottish general degree structure, the American liberal arts custom of adding course to course until a degree
could be claimed was familiar. Courses in graduate school and
comprehensive examinations were a new form of education. Un-
familiarity was complete when it came to the role of chairman.
However, I felt that I had been looked over pretty thoroughly.
I knew some of the people who had recommended me. I trusted
their judgment, and I had confidence in myself.

Without boasting, I had evidence to support my personal
"good conceit." Beginning with a degree from Queen's University, Belfast, there were a couple of research projects completed
and published, one in anthropology and one a field study of
rural depopulation.

At that time, I had acquaintance with the subject through
personal reading and the use of ideas from sociology in the design of research. Later, I was to undergo formal training in New
York and Chicago and to put this to work in further field research. The subject and myself seemed to attract each other: I
liked the brash, questioning activity displayed in sociological
papers and found my own research congenial in that the type of
explanation developed by sociologists fitted the problems that
I was trying to solve. After 1950, installed as the university lecturer in sociology at Oxford, I was an enthusiastic convert to the
new academic discipline. My role at Oxford was to break down
resistance to, and explore the nature of the demand for, instruction in the subject. Lectures by friends from the U.S.A. helped
greatly in this educational process. I saw to it that questions
were raised whenever appropriate, I taught the subject, and
above all I acted as consultant to aspirants for higher research
degrees, as well as engaging in some personal research, and all
this gradually built up pressure for change. I never considered
myself an Oxford type and did not get personal pleasure from

the formal pomp of dining at High Table in College. So, having completed two pieces of research and accumulated some good will for the subject, I was attracted to a job in the U.S.A. That the job was partly administrative rather than purely scholarly seemed to me a natural development of an academic career.

But the academic environment down South was hostile: we stood at the first party, and it seemed as stiff as an East-West encounter. Half the time, we thought of the warnings about living in the South that had poured over us in New York and by mail from Ohio and Colorado. For the other half, we went out to meet these new personalities, seeking, expecting, wishing for Southern warmth, hospitality, charm, ease, and grace. None could be found on that occasion; thus we learned that Southern formality was the upper side of the culture. Everybody there was as disappointed as we were but nobody could relax on spiced tea. Six weeks were to elapse before we were offered a drink at a party.

When I tried to find out what was expected of a chairman, no one seemed to want to talk. Colleagues looked me straight in the eye and said calmly, "Oh, you can do all that has to be done in an afternoon a week." Deans said, "Just read the instructions we send and keep to the deadlines and all will be well." Other chairmen were most evasive of all; they said the job is what you make it, you develop your own style. It all sounded so much like the cookbook instruction, "Place in a warm oven till done." Worse still, everybody dropped their voices and narrowed their eyes when the subject came up. Guarded looks and evasive words went together.

Considered as a social system separate from the town, the nearest parallel to the college I found myself in was a despotic royal court, say that of Charles I of England or Louis XVI of France; the fact that both those monarchs lost their heads is irrelevant. The chief of administration of the university acted like a monarch; and deans, department heads, and faculty were constrained to behave like courtiers. The accents were Southern and the motions were gracious; but underneath, individuals denied enough power and support to fulfill their roles showed their anxiety by ritualism or withdrawal. Styles of reaction became something to observe. No individual trusted more than one or two close cronies; card-playing groups met like English school prefects behind locked doors. Information from the administration building was closely guarded and passed only within certain circles; every bit had to be checked and counter-checked for accuracy; no one trusted anyone else, even a crony would let you down. Coffee groups abounded, but loyalties were such that to join one meant exclusion from others, not physical exclusion or anything so crude as that but exclusion from the information of vital import.

All this was evident in the first few weeks. My individualistic Scots-Irish background had built into my personality the sense that I was as good as the next chap; indeed I even felt that I was better at some things than most. However, the courtier had a legitimate style of life and, if need be, no doubt I could learn to give an adequate performance.

Beyond the courtiers and beyond the deans and beyond the faculty wives, whose secretarial-type jobs provided a useful informal leakage of administrative secrets, and beyond minor administrative personnel, two other groups are important to this history, the "influentials" and the "Northerners." The names have nothing to do with origins; they refer to attitudes only. It is true that most courtiers were Southern born and educated, most influentials Southern born but educated at Northern universities, and most Northerners both born and educated in the Northern or Western states. The division is not exact, for some courtiers were Northern migrants and some influentials were Southern educated; attitudes are more important than ecology at this place in the narrative. Between the magnolias outside the administrative building and Osage orange trees outside the faculty club on the campus were other faculty types: the professional country boys, the bouncing athletes, the loners of the library or the lab, and the literary segregationists.

At this point, I became aware that something was disturbing the system. The courtiers hissed secrets at each other, and strange noises were coming from other elements on the campus. The whole place was buzzing with one issue. It was at one, alive, vibrant, with everybody, even the loners, involved. From a state of anomie, the move toward complete integration had been so sudden it was like an explosion.

A senior dean sought my allegiance in a long, involved conference that obscured totally what the fuss was about. Faculty members tried to explain all the ramifications of the issue; careers were at stake, principles flouted, academic freedoms infringed, they said. Three separate manifestos were produced in my office, on each occasion after conversations designed to find out how I felt about the fundamental values of motherhood, decency, and the Independent American Spirit. One seemed to me to be more sensible than the others, so forgetting completely my resolve to play the role of courtier, I signed the paper.

Next thing I knew, the president and I were driving home together. I had been walking as usual across campus when coming round a magnolia tree we encountered each other casually. On the way, conversation turned to questions of university policy and development. The central issue of campus life was not mentioned. The president seemed to want answers to questions that had no precise meaning for me, except as broad areas for academic discussion on the working of organizations in general. His disappointment was perfectly obvious; he was never a man to hide his feelings. Though we often had appointments, we never did meet casually again.

In a week the dean who had brought me to the place was gone and a new one installed. The ride with the president had evidently given him grounds for a quick decision on me; my independence in signing a manifesto and my slowness to perceive the exact, local significance of words and attitudes in a fast-moving crisis unfitted me for the higher reaches of an administrative team.

By the end of the semester, a graduate student had been dismissed for failing to see the need for courtly deference to those in authority. The fact that he was a Northerner and had never "quite fitted in" was given to legitimatize the decision. That he was an excellent scholar, a good man in his community, and a pleasant person were acknowledged. Only half the faculty was sad he had to go; the manifesto signers and those who offered their resignations thought it was a disgrace both to the institution and to their association with it. That the dismissed student was a Negro got into no official communication; all informal conversation began and ended with that fact.

I went off to teach in a summer session to recoup the family

budget after our transatlantic removal, leaving the bitterness of
our new social system with some joy. Our own set of cronies,
whom we knew well, said farewell as if they never expected to
see us return. I wondered why they showed such anxiety; somehow, in spite of friendship ties, the strength of feelings they
showed seemed excessive.

In the fall, I had still to discover what a chairman was supposed to do. Decisions could no longer be postponed. My assignment was to build a department but my dean was gone, the
president had deserted me and, despite much effort, I still had
made little contact with my fellow chairmen.

As in any society, everyone on campus played many roles and
could be classified accurately for different purposes as a member
of several groups. So some chairmen were campus influentials,
some were not; all chairmen were courtiers of necessity some of
the time, but some were courtiers all the time and never influentials. Consequently, there was no single group of chairmen. Indeed the one thing all chairmen were convinced about was that
administrative policy consisted of *divide et impera*. So I never
did meet my fellow chairmen *qua* chairmen; any attempt to get
such a group together would have been construed as treachery.

Starting from first principles, reading the files in my office
(which stopped recording events three years before I arrived),
asking direct questions of near office neighbors about specific
problems, I progressed through the winter. Budget season was
the worst; pressures from colleagues seemed no greater than expected. The new dean was pleasantly co-operative. We discussed
policies and personalities with candor. Later, after the budget
had been approved and most of my needs had been overlooked,
I went back. It seemed to me to be discourteous and ungentle-
manly to behave in this fashion, but I discovered it was normal.
Chairmen were handed out orders and apparently had to live
as best they could with whatever explanation they could devise.
So I learned another lesson in adjustment.

One most significant conversation took place over lunch. I
was boxed in at table by a bevy of four influentials. We settled
the problems of the United Nations over the main course, and
produced a solution for American foreign policy in the Mediter-
ranean over the dessert. Around us football phrases and snatches

floated up from others at the table but we five had our heads together and turned, over the coffee, to the Southern way of life. I was shattered to find on all four sides people who believed passionately in Negro inferiority, in the rightness of color segregation, and who identified the South as the only place in the United States that had a clear concept of the gentleman. These influentials were Northern by birth and upbringing; so clearly here is a case where converts to a system of beliefs express them more strongly than those who learned them more slowly in the family circle.

The influence of those beliefs quaintly known as the "Southern way of life" completely pervaded the general atmosphere. However, the oddest thing to take about living in this atmosphere was that for the most part the pleasantest people were segregationists. My table companions were nasty about it, but, if you could steer other Southerners away from their moral guilt and anxiety, on every other topic they were excellent company. There were so many of them it would have been strange if no congenial intellects were to be found.

The liberals, by and large, were a weak lot, inclined to be defensive, suspicious of degrees of commitment, evasive and unimpressive even when they stood up staunchly for values you could approve. They were a low-status out-group and as such riven with dissents over this issue or that one. Some few were magnificent; they had maintained a sense of integrity without feeling any personal antagonism. We shall always count ourselves fortunate to have known one or two of them.

A call from the president, about a year after my chance automobile ride with him, placed me squarely on the carpet. He was furious. A faculty member had appeared in court as an expert witness in a racial case. Neither his academic freedom nor his rights as a citizen were in question. But a clever segregationist lawyer had made him look ridiculous, and the president was in a rage. I believe the intent was to ask me to take the stand to correct this unfortunate impression but by this time I could be a diplomat when necessary and so we mutually avoided taking any decision on the matter.

As a foreigner trying to be recognized as a member of the administrative team, these were striking episodes. Less conspicuous was the constant defense that was necessary. Innocent and not so innocent colleagues presented me as an Englishman. Now, the stereotypes conjured up by this word in this Southern college are not good; they are a combination of pomposity and contempt for local customs evinced by visiting lecturers. Not to mention the last faculty member from England who charmed everyone but went off after a semester, leaving thousands of dollars in unpaid debts. Consequently, I and my family waged a struggle to be recognized as British, not English; recognition meant that after two years on the faculty only personal enemies kept raising the foreigner issue, and querying if we were paying our fair share in income tax. Again the Northerners and liberals were most apt to drop references to Perfidious Albion; we took this as a sign of their own feelings of inadequate acceptance.

Even more objectionable was the training issues. In a professional discipline in the U.S.A. it is apparently customary to demand item-by-item course work before colleague acceptance is complete; so, for instance, no one should teach population analysis without a course in population. The fact that one has written and used the techniques is merely evidence of precocity, but really acceptable skill requires the personal blessings of some instructor or other. For teaching, in particular, such an *imprimatur* claims to be essential. One wonders with amusement where all the new courses that are presented each year at faculty meetings can originate.

Now, I had chosen my subject, sociology, at the mature age of thirty-three. William Ogburn taught me when we worked together for two years in England that sociology should be thought of as a science and not as a set of scholastic doctrines. Acceptance of concepts or propositions depended on evidence; achievement counted, not the label that goes with attendance at a particular place. So all the emphasis on one set of trainees being relocated from a graduate university to college campuses for the purpose of reproducing the courses they had attended, seemed to me to be muddled thinking if not downright pernicious. Training was widely propagated as a device in this college for keeping things as they were believed to have been. Thus, in spite of being fairly well known in the profession, I found myself being treated like an infidel in Mecca.

All I wanted was peace to discover how to be a good chairman, and some little support once I had set new goals. The old had been clearly inadequate or I should not have been where I was. Neither peace nor support was easily attained. Snipers shot anti-foreigner darts and anti-science arrows all weekend at cocktail parties. It was good fun to unmask them at this task. Support depended on the campus influentials and tolerance from someone in the administration. Here no humor was possible; life was grim; relenting had no part in their scheme of things.

The point is that I had to learn to react positively to others' perceptions of me, that is, to see myself with the eyes of an alien culture. I was confident enough to think that I need not defend my preparation, my reputation, my image. I knew I had not come to the U.S.A. as a penniless refugee, glad to be rescued. I came voluntarily, welcoming a new opportunity, proud of my academic record. I expected this to be known and saw it as a duty of my academic sponsors to do this. Unfortunately, this behavior was not part of this culture where every man was his own sponsor.

Exhortations to leave the ivory tower and mingle in community affairs were made on annual occasions of high solemnity as in the ceremonial welcome to new faculty. It occurred to me after hearing this twice that given some federal funds, the community might welcome a research enquiry. So I made contact with two major institutions and explained what my research ideas involved. They promised immediate and wholehearted cooperation and provided an interesting set of related problems to which they wanted some solutions. All this was explained within the university, and again blessings were pronounced on the whole operation.

Washington, too, consulted in quintuplicate by pink, white, green, yellow, and blue papers carrying identical messages, offered all that had been asked. Up to this, the incident is an administrative success. All had gone so smoothly there was half a year left before any work need begin. The dean and I met with a federal representative to iron out a few final budget points. This was to be a co-operative research contract with the university finding around 20 per cent of the budget. It took an afternoon of explanation to clear up what seemed to me a simple formula in accountancy and one, moreover, that had already been accepted. There was a reluctance to meet commitments verbally made in another office. With a good deal of fussing, the budget items were laid out line by line. Every detail of the contract was finally ready for signature. Now, I can see that both parties to one of these contracts must know exactly what is implied, but explanations can be overdrawn.

The research contract was never in fact signed. The community was tolerant; the department was eager; the administration was prepared to permit the work to begin. But the federal announcement that no more segregated housing could be built ruined a good research design. The city was not ready to build under the new conditions, and before they eventually overcame their reluctance, we were committed to a change of residence ourselves.

As the second year rolled around, my memories of the first led me to make very extensive inquiries on procedures and expectations. At this time, too, pressures from inside and outside the college led to the early resignation of the president. The new leader would take over in the new year after a nine-month interregnum.

Throughout this power vacuum, appointments made represented the rescue of a friend from deeper in the South. While this type of appointment policy is admirable as a device for maintaining academic departmental lineages, it does not lead to cross-fertilization of ideas, nor to greatness. Departures too often represented creative individuals whose unwillingness to conform had earned them the dread title of troublemaker. Men active in research and publishing were allowed to take offers elsewhere; teaching and training triumphed over research; regional loyalties became stronger than before.

My summer assignments became more and more important to survival. "Western University" campus had also in the intervening year experienced a revolution. Our June arrival coincided with a remarkable series of ceremonies: academic "wakes" with *keens* for departing deans, and then a month later huzzahs of welcome for the new administrative team. Western campus has a different atmosphere; there was a solid academic base. People who had tenure felt secure, although administrators came and went. Tenure in the South, without the approbation of the local in-groups, merely meant the capacity to ignore verbal and salary assaults. I suppose the difference between the two institutions is basically that in the South faculty loyalty to each other is low, while in the West it is high. The Western faculty also had a real role to play in setting academic policies. Finally, at Western University chairmen were elected by their departments and acted as their agents. At Southern they were courtiers or else agents of central administration sent out to colonize and control academic territories.

The Lesson Learned

In this brief account of our reactions to the academic and social environment in the South, we have deliberately chosen to exclude individual personality differences. We grew to love and to trust some individuals; we found we could work with others, but as for some, the less said the better. While it is customary to write about institutions as carrying the stamp of the men who inhabit them, the *assimilando* in the South finds that he is on test by a whole culture. The culture is a way of life, that is to say, a set of goals, a set of social interdependencies through which such goals are to be reached, and a set of rules which govern the relations between individuals. From this standpoint, the uniqueness of each personality has less importance than the common web of beliefs that links them together into a system of norms and actions.

Within the social system of the college, the role of the chairman has a central position in the web of interdependencies. It connects the college, as a device for teaching particular individuals, with the faculty. The faculty through its teaching and research proclaims the distillate of the universals of human culture. So the chairman has the task of making arrangements whereby particular students are brought face to face with the wisdom of mankind. In a regional setting, under the eye of alumni and administration that respect a local community culture, this can expose a chairman to pressure.

We can see him as a conductor with the departmental faculty as performers. The administration sets broad goals such as to match the highest quality of thought or to provide complete

academic freedom. It is within the task of the chairman to choose
players and translate these abstract goals into actual behavior. As
with a good conductor, support from a staff who see to the
audience, collect admission fees, and supervise rooms and timetables is essential. The analogy must not be pressed too far
because even a small college will have fifteen to twenty departments, and the metaphor of the single orchestra with its own
conductor leads to confusion.

Another image of the chairman sees him as a committee man.
In this case he keeps the records, writes the letters, and acts as
representative for the group. In action with other departments
or with the administration of the college, he may play his part
as a delegate. He is the spokesman for decisions made collectively
in departmental meetings and has no freedom of action. He may
alternatively play the role of representative as a trustee for the
department. This gives him considerable freedom of decision
and must be based on trust and confidence built up in his decisions over a number of years.

All this discussion assumes that a chairman speaks for his department as a leader of a team. Another standpoint is that of the
administration who may see the chairman as their representative,
a colonial governor dispatched to rule over an outlying academic
territory. In the college I chose to join, this was the normal
image of the chairman. So, most began their reign as outsiders;
at each succession the old faculty was sacked with little respect
for tenure and new men appointed. Loyalties between established campus influentials and the long-established administrative officers were too dangerous to a newcomer to be left intact.
For, as we have emphasized, in Southern University there was a
single source of power, the president. Pressure on the president
from alumni or parents found expression in a direct fashion,
often bypassing deans and department heads and reaching individual faculty members. Such visitations were rare but as dev-
astating as an earthquake in a peaceful valley. Normally, the
system operated smoothly enough even if most people always
metaphorically glanced over their shoulder at each move.

At Southern University the administration faced tremendous
problems that threatened to disrupt several of its major schools.
Ideas of academic freedom, of student rights, and of citizen rights

held by faculty, alumni, students, and administrators were in violent conflict. To build a department, a new head has to attract attention and support. At a time when key personnel of the administrative team were losing power and being replaced, the department could not get this attention.

Without this freedom to begin completely anew, any successor has to be protected by forces outside his department until he establishes himself. This support can only come from administrators. Within a college system a strong department can do nothing to help a weak one. We now know cases where a single department head is larger in terms of money and manpower than the rest of the college he inhabits. Obviously this is not good for the equilibrium of the college. A good administration would seek to hold a fair balance in all its departments.

The transition from being a teacher to being a chairman is nowhere more traumatic than in the value given to information. As a teacher, giving information in accessible amounts and in a palatable form is a major good. This fits in conformably with the general value that the "right to know" is guaranteed to every U.S. citizen; the deliberate withholding of knowledge in this context could almost be considered an un-American activity.

The chairman discovers at once that information is not freely available; to know a little more of what is going on than the next chap is power. So the chairman moves into a world of classified information, of secrets which may be passed on but not attributed, and of taboo areas which may never be revealed. Equals in status may differ in the amount of information they obtain and thus differ in their capacity to influence events. It is in this area of adaptation to the social environment that familiarity with the affective language of gestures and cues special to the system gives a tremendous advantage. Probably this explains why long-term residents in a college often make the best junior administrators like chairmen and deans.

In the mixture of undergraduate and graduate teaching and research that make up any college, the career of chairman is both simple and complex. The simple aspect concerns routine administrative detail of courses, timetables, duties, and academic standards of performance. The complex aspects are the problems of setting goals with a limited number of degrees of freedom and collecting enough resources from foundations or federal funds to set in motion plans to achieve them.

The styles in behavior and attitude appropriate to the role of chairman differ according to the nature of the college. We have now seen in operation colleges with different types of social structure, such as a well-established bureaucratic hierarchy, an open, free-for-all refugee-type social system, and a single totalitarian rule. Under a tyranny, only courtiers can survive. In an open social system, preference goes to the entrepreneur or the strong-minded, inner-directed type of chairman. The bureaucracy type of college values harmony between departments, balance above brilliance, and selects those who are co-operative rather than purely competitive. So, while in America I have become assimilated to the administrative system. I have learned to welcome the excitement of fast-moving events, to live with hostility and still find its curbs amusing. I have learned that to administer is to control, that is, to set goals and keep records of progress towards them, to help members to adapt to each other and get maximum enjoyment from what has to be done for the common goal. But who knows what I would have learned during the same number of years while in Britain?

WILLIAM T. LIU

The Confucian Scholar
and the American Dream

AMONG the foreign-born scholars in American universities and research institutes, those from the Far East have come to represent one of the largest group; among the latter, the Chinese intellectual has not only gained particularly much in numbers, but has also pre-empted what novelty and prestige remain in being a Confucian scholar. Many people, colleagues and outsiders alike, still view him as the Confucian disciple of the old days who sets himself apart from the populace. He is the inscrutable man, dedicated to ideas but not to action; he spends his days studying the classics of ancient China; and he is somewhat lonely. While his wife sympathizes with his intellectual pursuits, she does not share his activities, and he himself rarely, if ever, renders her the spousal help in rocking the bassinet or fixing the curtain rod.

This stereotype might have been true in the past, but is definitely false in the present. Chinese scholarship in general has gone through some historical changes because scholarship is always changeable and because China as a country has seen more innovations in this century than during many previous centuries of her history.

Around 1919 in China occurred the May Fourth Movement (or, as it is called, the Chinese Cultural Renaissance) which displaced the formerly staid and authoritarian atmosphere of the country's scholarship with a more robust intellectual, romantic, and utilitarian spirit. After that, students in China came to identify themselves with the learning and freedom of the West. A new pattern of thinking emerged. The Western thought and the rejection of Confucian tradition were regarded as signs of scholarship and patriotism, and Western learning was viewed as a sure way to improve one's chances in an increasingly crowded job market or to prepare for academic careers. The old civil service examination system had been abolished, but no new mechanism had been found for electing the elect, although academic learning continued to be the most respected vocation. Under these circumstances, a Western education became the magic symbol of social prestige, and the Chinese youth considered schooling in one of the Western countries as the foremost goal of their ambition. So they set out, amidst hope and inexperience, on what proved to be a long and devious journey, leading some of them eventually to a lasting residence in America.

The statement that Chinese scholars in America reject the traditional learning of China and find a personal renaissance in the Western scientific and technological tradition is a truism that does not penetrate very deeply into the actualities influencing their mode of adjustment. Each Chinese scholar who discusses his American experience has a vested interest in expressing satisfaction and pride in his education. When he says, "I started out in my intellectual career as an idealist but learned from the American system that I'd better be a pragmatist," it is like saying, "I have discovered an entirely new type of learning." At the same time, my own years in America have led me to believe that identification with Western scholarship does not necessarily give a person high esteem in the eyes of his colleagues, nor does adherence to Chinese classics impress others as being profound. Rather, these opposing tendencies represent stages in a process which is slow and subtle even for the sharpest minds—to find one's way into a system of thought.

The best way to understand the American experience of Chinese scholars is to contrast those who came before World War II with those who came after. The former came to this country mainly on that indemnity money which the American government, following the Boxer Rebellion at the end of the last century, made available for the education of Chinese students abroad. Because of the general awakening of the intellectual class after the shame of being defeated by the West and because of the age-old system of awards, those whom the Chinese government chose for further education in America were generally bright and dedicated. They were selected by the scholar-bureaucrats of China as men of promise and purpose and sent out on a mission—to learn the Western political and economic system, bring their new learning back to the home country, and reform the old system that prevailed there.

Those who were selected for this mission had the goal of changing the intellectual traditions of China, but at the same time, they were like the other scholars of the country and closely adhered to the traditions of the old order. Their dilemma was aggravated by the fact that the ruling bureaucracy, too, was pulled both by the desire to change and the will to persist. Such a situation naturally limited their American experience. For all the talk about the conversion of the earlier Chinese scholars in America to Western ideals and about their role as intellectual agents in Chinese society, their conversion seems to have been rather superficial. The newly acquired ideas and values did not, as a rule, penetrate their daily lives, and the Western sentiments could not filter through the intimate network of their social relationships. Both to their American roommates at Columbia, Harvard, and Michigan and to their Chinese kin and associates, the American-educated Chinese remained basically Chinese.

In the course of a few years in America they did all they could to learn the science, logic, mathematics, rhetoric, and social and political thought of the West. Then, having completed their education, they returned to China and eventually assumed political and social responsibilities. Their impact was great. By creating their own newspapers and magazines, they introduced the Chinese to the writings of Oscar Wilde and Ezra Pound and to the political philosophies of Jefferson and Lincoln as well; at the same time, they introduced the West to the works of ancient China translated into English. The vernacular language and literature movement, highlighted later by the Chinese Renaissance of 1919, was led largely by Chinese students in America, of whom Hu Shih has been the moving spirit.

Persuading the Chinese public to accept the new views was a painfully frustrating experience, bound to create tensions. Thus a measure of tension developed between the scholar who returned from America and those who adhered to the old traditions. Further tensions developed within the American-educated elite class, the majority of which followed the traditional career and entered government service. For them, the reward of gaining public offices and the prestige accompanying their positions offset the feeling of frustration; these people came to identify themselves with the destiny of the society and to consider themselves the guardians of tradition. But those American-educated scholars who for some reason did not take positions in the government became alienated, powerless and self-estranged. Serious though they seemed to be, the purpose of their activities, for better or worse, gradually became centered upon intellectual creativity as an end in itself.

What has been said so far is intended to demonstrate that, except for a very few, the Chinese scholars entered into intellectual life neither from a really deep desire to pursue scientific endeavors nor from a commitment to sustain and transmit the complex traditions of the free intellectuals. Rather, they saw themselves as the guardians of the moral fabric of society and as the custodians of a vast administrative machinery. In this sense they were politicians and bureaucrats.

We probably will never know what personal motives moved those Chinese scholars who elected to remain in America; it is possible that a large number of them did so in spite of themselves. In any case, it seems to me, we can distinguish three types among them. The first consists of those who, because of their former political affiliations, could find suitable positions in neither the Nationalist nor the Communist government and established their existence in America as lecturers and writers. Ironically enough, their fortunes greatly changed with the collapse of the Nationalist regime on the mainland. This was the time when many famous research and graduate centers in America initiated China-area studies, offering new opportunities to those who were versatile in such problems. The Chinese scholar of this type required, perhaps, a few months of hard work to refresh his knowledge and brush up his academic routine that he had learned during the 1930's at Michigan or Harvard; with that, he became a Chinese specialist within the academic setting, a scholar in a fast-growing, timely field. Thus, their primary reason for staying in America has been more political and familial than economic. They have been appropriately described by Paul Siu as *sojourners* whose adjustment to America is never quite complete because, in order to capitalize on their background as a professional qualification, they wish people to think of them as being totally Chinese.

The second type consists of those who, because of similar reasons, took up work in an international field such as missionary work or cross-cultural communication of ideas. In order to perform their duties effectively, it is imperative that they have a certain professional commitment to the standard of their work. Accordingly, intellectual endeavor is to them only a prerequisite for doing their work well; their real aim lies in their commitment to social and economic action. They find it neither essential nor beneficial to take the role of a Chinese in their public and professional life, although by doing so they add the color of liberal internationalism to the institution to which they belong. Their behavioral model lies not with their Chinese identity, nor with the intellectual community, but with the spirit of internationalism which their institution fosters.

The third group consists of those who, having neither the experience of the first group nor the purposes of the second, find an alternative symbol of success: money. Their educational preparation had not given them skills in demand by the host society that would have insured them a more or less stable place in the professions. For those who lacked such skills there was an abundance of business opportunities promising success. One cannot help but notice, especially in the large seaboard cities of America, the number of Chinese scholars who have become entrepreneurial-minded. The diversification of their talents and business activities may be equaled only by the Chinese in Southeast Asia.

These scholars-turned-businessmen found their newly acquired wealth less helpful in making a social success than, say, immigrants from Europe did. The competitive structure of the American business system inevitably molded their temperaments and sharpened up their shrewd, business-like approach to life. Beneath the skin, however, they preserved the typical traits of the Chinese—a certain clannishness and a system of values that is anything but puritanical. Since during their younger years in academic circles, they have acquired a special respect for scholarship and the fine arts, they occasionally attempt to compose poetry or write an essay for Chinese magazines. In addition, most of their acquaintances are still in the circle of Chinese scholars and the strong ties with their ivy tower peers continue to bring them back to the group of people with whom this paper is concerned.

Suddenly, after World War II, a new kind of Chinese scholar began to arrive in the United States. They were mainly young men who apparently came for an advanced degree in a major graduate school of the country. Were they graduate students in spite of themselves? Prior to 1953, at which time the Refugee Relief Act enabled many students from mainland China to become residents of the United States, the uncertainty of the State Department's policy concerning the status of Chinese students and refugees compelled most of these young men to stay in school. As they continued to take a full load of graduate courses, many suddenly found themselves being named to candidacy for a Ph.D. degree; all that was left to be done was to write up the results of a project on which they had already spent a number of years.

In 1955, when visiting a big Midwestern state university, I was told about one advanced course in the engineering department where the enrollment consisted of seven Chinese and one American, and the professor reportedly stated in the classroom that his excursion into Chinatown was most exciting. Several years later, Professor Philip M. Hauser of the University of Chicago said that among 17 students in one of his advanced seminars, 15 were Asian and two were Americans so that the latter were dubbed as "poor foreigners."

Graduate students are a small minority in the campus population of the country. Among the Chinese students in America, however, the reverse is true, mainly because the majority had already completed undergraduate work in the Far East before they came to the United States. Once here, they set their goals at the Master's level, but, after one or two years in school, the Ph.D. degree seemed to be within easy reach, and the continuation of their education became a matter of course rather than a matter of scholarly commitment. In the United States there were many job opportunities such as are not available in the Far East;

but in order to stay in the United States, the young Chinese needed a certificate of full-time student status.

If he happened to be in a field where there were numerous graduate fellowships, he could easily combine work and study; if his field was less fortunate, he could look for employment outside the campus. And so the Chinese student was able to establish an existence for himself which was penurious but not void of its pleasures and satisfactions. Within the confines of the campus and following the standard of living of the graduate students, he could live on $50.00 a week, support a wife and a child, drive a used car, much the same way as the other families in the graduate students' housing quarters did. He could even indulge in increasing his comfort and buying the couch of his neighbor who had graduated and was leaving to take a job. His sense of deprivation was offset by a vision of the future full of untold opportunities. A siege of flu, a burnt-out clutch, or an unexpected expense would not precipitate a mental crisis, but rather helped to assimilate him into the American way of life.

He now began to share the anxiety, hope, and rhythm of life of the other graduate students; typing papers while their wives fed the baby; paying the automobile repair bill in monthly installments; and eating hamburgers as the regular diet. The rhythm of the academic semester helped him along, and the vacations gave him a chance to regroup his forces and retreat with his family for a stretch of relatively relaxed living. Then, too, there were other students from the Far East who would visit and share the meals of native cuisine. The written quarterly and monthly reports required by the immigration authorities were now routine matters. The Chineses student's goal was, by this time, clear and well-defined—to complete his thesis, find a job, and become a part of the great American dream.

I have sketched the career of the Chinese scholars according to the time of their immigration, but time is by no means the only factor that helps to explain their problem. An equally important factor is the attitude that the Chinese scholar takes towards himself—his self-conception and identification with people and ideas. If he identifies himself with the bureaucratic structure of old China, his present problem in America is to justify himself in light of the new political regime. His work in scholarship becomes much like the work of a lawyer who meticulously prepares his case by presenting more and more evidence to support his position and seldom, if ever, entertains alternative arguments. His work becomes, rather than an original creation, a series of critiques of the present and, as it happens more frequently, of the past. He may do painstaking work in search of information to strengthen his argument; he may uncover new material and develop new concepts. But his desire to follow the intellectual tradition of the West by accepting and analyzing contradicting views is usually subordinated to his original commitment and conviction.

If he wishes to identify himself with the intellectual class in America, his main problem is to bridge the eternal gap between the Chinese and the Western traditions of scholarship. During his education to become a scholar he bypassed that area of learning which constitutes the core of the Western intellectual heritage, and later in life he is not likely to make up for what he missed. While his American colleagues show a natural versatility in the Western classics, appropriately quoting Plato, Shakespeare, and Freud, his contribution to the cocktail-party conversation is often limited to a presentation of Mencius' view of human nature; and this is usually all that his colleagues expect of him.

Whether he likes it or not, he is, in the daily routine of his work and in the daily presentation of his self, forced into the role of being a Chinese scholar, with the accent on "Chinese" rather than "scholar." After all, he can never entirely hide his Mongoloid racial traits and can hardly obscure his cultural and ethnic identity. But in a world oriented toward scientific and technological achievement, he can stress the technical competence of his scholarship and expect prestige and success as due rewards. It is therefore understandable that his desire to identify himself with the impersonal and sometimes rigid demands of his profession is stronger than that of his American colleagues.

The recent tendency among Chinese scholars to pursue their careers in the pure and natural sciences as well as in engineering can be explained by their search for a goal, in which they can find the gratification of equal achievements with their American colleagues. The criteria used to evaluate achievement in the precise sciences are more concrete and objective than any-where else. Anxious for security and pushed by the desire to stay in America, the Chinese scholar is necessarily drawn toward re-search work where procedure weighs more than information, where irrelevancy can be disguised by logical arguments, and where a sometimes deceptive elegance brings startling new order to the disturbing chaos of raw-sense experiences.

In 1960, a publication listing the doctoral theses submitted by Chinese scholars in American universities showed that the dissertations completed prior to World War II were mainly in the humanities and social sciences, while those completed after the last war were, in their overwhelming majority, in science, engineering, and life sciences. Kung in a more recent volume, *Chinese in American Life,* reports that of about twelve hundred Chinese faculty members in American universities and colleges, more than 70 per cent are in physical and natural sciences, in-cluding medicine, agricultural sciences, and engineering. On the other hand, the combined total in the humanities and social sciences comprise only about 20 per cent of the whole. The re-mainder is distributed among education, business administra-tion, music, etc.

My argument is not the point that Chinese scholars are ori-ented towards technical and instrumental fields of scholarship rather than towards normative and socio-emotional disciplines of which the social sciences and humanities are a part. True enough, even among those Chinese scholars who engage in social sciences, the tendency is to identify with empirical research rather than with speculative and historical methods. My argu-ment is that the difference between those who engage in pure and natural sciences and those who are in humanities and social sciences seems to lie in the individual's perception of his oppor-tunity as a Chinese scholar in the professional job market. Most of those who are engaged in humanities and social sciences are given teaching assignments in fields dealing with Chinese or other non-Western cultures. Whether this trend has come about by design or by chance, such academic specialization always seems to reflect the individual's Chinese origin rather than his scholarly competence. Therefore, I argue, one latent but important reason for entering careers in science and engineering is to avoid the stigma of being a Chinese scholar.

Intellectual recognition in itself is not enough to satisfy a person's social and emotional needs. The integration process always has a non-professional dimension also which poses its own problems. The majority of Chinese scholars are still more at home with their former compatriots. Their cultural and racial identity delimit the invisible enclave within which their activities are carried on. Those who came with their families, of course, have problems quite different from those who came single. The latter are exposed to the whole complex of a previously unexperienced dating and courtship routine of the West. A single man must learn how to lead a life in a metropolitan center in which he is viewed and treated as an alien and a Chinaman. His professional and technical competence does not greatly improve his bargaining position in the fiercely competitive dating market. He can improve his appearance with the aid of tailored suits and the devices of the national toiletry industry. He may attain a superior earning power; yet, in spite of all these, his field for hunting a mate is small for two reasons. First, there is the racial difference, which in some states of the country presents a legal problem. Secondly, his academic background and occupational life limit his range of choice to the college-educated members of the opposite sex.

The social pressures to get married and settle down to family life are just as strong on the young Chinese than on any young American, but the chances are not the same. The young Chinese has poorer chances right at the beginning, and as he grows older the chances constantly decrease. Eventually, he becomes less discriminating in his choice and, if he ever marries, his decision is likely to be motivated by reason rather than by romantic love. There are some interesting data hidden in the *Annual Report* of the American Immigration and Naturalization Service suggesting that the alien Chinese married American citizens more often as a means of obtaining legal residence in America than as a means of satisfying their personal need for companionship and love. The *Report* shows that marriages between Chinese immigrants and U.S. citizens increased from nearly zero in 1946 to 195 in 1948, the year when the Communists began their conquest of mainland China. By 1949, the number rose to 235, and in 1952 to 490. But after the Emergency Refugee Act of 1953 permitted the entry of Chinese refugees to America, the number of Chinese marrying U.S. citizens plummeted to 158 in 1954, even though the group of marriageable males had increased since 1948.

But let us not attribute more wisdom to statistical data than they really have. The question that I often ask myself is beyond statistics: What are the implications of being a Chinese in these United States? To this, the old stereotype of the Confucian scholar gives a wrong answer indeed. It might be true, as it is often said, that the Chinese student comes to this country with his basic character set like a plaster and, however anxious he is to become Americanized, he remains a Chinese. But the inevitable course of his life must be determined also by his professional identity, which gives his existence an additional meaning. As a professional, being exploited by the competitive nature of his academic job and subjected to emotional dislocations by his pride and sense of shame, success and failure, he comes to compromise with the idea that the deeper questions of personal purpose are not worth pondering. As his career proceeds, he becomes more narrowly respectable in his style of life and level of intellectual exercise, he experiences the melting pot of America and fits himself into an intellectual community. Then it does not matter any more whether he still possesses a capacity for worldly salvation, a grasp of the time and the culture to which he once belonged.

After all, it might be that the Confucian scholar has never been unearthly and inscrutable, or there are no Confucian scholars in present-day America. And again, it might be that America is inscrutable and modern life imposes upon us many more problems than the human mind can solve.

JOSEPH S. ROUCEK

Between Radicalism and Respectability

The Fate of the Emigré and His Political Ideas

THE UNITED STATES has always been a haven for refugees who were unable to achieve their political aims in their homelands or were driven across the border by political changes. The personal vicissitudes of these émigrés have been often written up by devoted historians or loyal members of an ethnic group; yet the question—relevant for the majority of Americans but less significant for the ethnic public—has been seldom asked: What was the influence of these émigrés, and of those ideas and doctrines that they brought along, upon American life and political philosophy?

These were essentially non-scholarly men but represented, sometimes on a popular and other times on a very academic level, philosophies and ideologies which they wholeheartedly attempted to teach to the masses and intellectuals in America. Hence, answers to my question can be found in many historical studies on the political movements of the past where they appear as passing references in the discussion of a tangential topic. Such partial answers deserve our attention because they are likely to express what the public opinion thinks. For example, in the work of an astute student of American nativism I find the following summary judgment:

> Since the flexibility of American institutions has continued to discourage extreme dissent, America's most uncompromising radicals have in fact come from abroad. This persistent contrast between a generally hopeful psychology of mobility in America and the more desperate politics born in class-ridden Europe has fostered the belief that violent

and sweeping opposition to the status quo is characteristically European and profoundly un-American. Thus, anti-
radical movements in America have had a singular propensity to assume a nationalistic form.[1]

The thesis is cogent and convincing, and any reader may recall
events of American history which seem to lend support to it. At
the same time, however, one cannot entirely forget the immigrant
compatriots of the political refugees who came from poor economic conditions and with little education, but achieved in
America success in terms of economic and social respectability.
If the thesis holds up, there must have been two kinds of immigrants coming to our shores: common folk who were not interested in the higher aspects of life and made respectable success,
and émigré intellectuals who relinquished hopeful respectability
for the sake of their radical ideas. While this apt summary of the
public opinion sounds plausible enough, I discover in it a certain suspicion directed against the refugee, émigré, or perhaps
the foreign-born intellectual in general, a suspicion which pin-
points him as the persistent carrier of un-American, radical ideas.
I do not intend to write an apologia of the suspected intellectual,
but somehow I find it hard to believe that the émigré would be
vastly different from his common-folk countrymen and would
be ready to renounce persistently the very human goals of respectability—unless powerful motives force him to do so. Accordingly, I find it hard to believe that the same émigré would ever
have been able to make a radical impact upon the political
thinking of America or to marshal such a political force as could
have threatened the status quo in this country. This is why I
propose to investigate the political refugees—their careers as well
as teachings—to see how well they fitted the American image of
foreign-born radicals.

We do not need to go back to the figures of General Lafayette,
Thaddeus Kosciusko, Casimir Pulaski, Thomas Paine, Alexander
Hamilton and others of foreign birth whose names became in-
separably linked to the independence and constitution of the
country. It is a moot question whether or not they were radicals

---

[1] John Higham, *Strangers in the Land* (New Brunswick, N.J.: Rutgers University Press, 1955), pp. 7-8.

when compared to other people of their epoch because whatever doctrines they professed, those doctrines contributed to the formation and basic institutions of America. They cannot be measured because they became the measures of Americanism for future generations.

The historical origins of our problem, however, take us back to the time of the fathers of the Constitution. The first outstanding problem calling attention to the influence of political refugees arose in connection with the Alien and Sedition Acts and was associated with the name of President John Adams as well as a number of immigrant scholars. Adams, whom Madison once described as "of ticklish temper," displayed shortly after his election his "ticklishness" about the Republican attacks on him and his administration. As chance had it, he felt especially imposed upon by a number of foreign-born people, many of whom were of fame and achievement, and all of whom appeared as aliens to the anglophile Federalist and descendant of an old Massachusetts family. Among those who could be labeled as aliens were the Swiss-born Albert Gallatin, who upon Madison's retirement from Congress had become Republican leader of the House; the English radical, Thomas Cooper, who had come to America in 1794 and soon proved himself as a vigorous Republican pamphleteer; a number of recently arrived French intellectuals, including the chemist Pierre A. Adet, the botanist Andre Michaux, and Victor du Pont, whom Adams suspected of being engaged in espionage. The same label was even more appropriate for many undistinguished French Jacobins who had fled the repression of the Directory and were now setting up a clamor against Adams, as well as for the defeated fighters of Irish freedom, a group most offensive to the anglophile Federalists, who chose this time to carry their insatiable hatred of Britain to the United States.

Adams' party had all these people in mind when they pushed through Congress a series of measures known as the Alien and Sedition Acts. The new laws were clearly designed for the purpose of restricting the political activities of the foreign-born. They raised the residence requirement for American citizenship; they empowered the President to order in peacetime any alien from the country and jail those who refused to go; they empowered him to jail in wartime any enemy alien at his pleasure; and, finally, they provided severe penalties for anyone speaking, writing, or publishing "with the intent to defame or bring into contempt or disrepute" the President or other members of the government.

The laws were passed at a time when it was thought that a strong link existed between foreign influences and domestic factions, but the same laws could also be used, and were used, for the repression of political opposition. Matthew Lyon, the outspoken Irish-born Republican congressman from Vermont was the first to be imprisoned, although during his jail term he was re-elected to Congress. All told, Federalist judges jailed and fined 70 people under the Sedition Act, and their case became a major campaign issue in the election year of 1800. The Republicans triumphed and eventually captured the Presidency and the control of Congress.

With this turn of political fortunes the Alien and Sedition Acts became short-lived measures and discreditable acts of power politics, but they left behind their lasting effect upon the mentality of the nation. They established, and perhaps sanctioned, a pattern of thinking which connected the name of the alien with the threat of sedition and envisaged the immigrant as an exponent of radicalism. Ever since, this pattern of thinking survived in America. Its hold over minds has from time to time greatly changed, alternating between popularity and oblivion. It has never become general and never extinct either; it has revived after oblivion, and at times of popularity it has caused national divisions just as it did in Adams' years.

In the early 1800's the anti-alien feelings subsided or, perhaps, adjusted themselves to those new problems involving refugees and their political activities that the historical events on both sides of the Atlantic produced. One type of a problem was created by the arrival of the Irish and their organizational activities on behalf of the Irish cause; another type of problem was presented by the Forty-eighters and the mass immigration of well-educated people.

From early times on, the influence of the immigrant was quite marked in local politics, and this factor could be often utilized by émigrés for initiating agitation in support of their European-based issues. The Irish, helped by their strategic location in the cities of the North Atlantic states, proved to be particularly ingenuous in assuming an active role in community politics and then applying their local experiences to the establishment of ethnic organizations favoring Irish causes. During the struggle for Catholic emancipation in Ireland in the 1820's, the Irish-American associations, and particularly the Friends of Ireland, sent money and encouragement to the Catholic Association in Dublin. A little while later Daniel O'Connell's repeal agitation secured even more Irish-American support; the repeal associations formed in many American cities collected a "rent" of twelve cents a month from their members for transmission to Ireland, and a National Repeal Convention held in New York in 1834 attracted delegates from thirteen states. The Young Ireland movement and the numerous Irish nationalist clubs of the 1850's followed a similar organizational scheme, establishing close co-operation between the Irish settlements in America and the specific organizations in Ireland.

For a hundred years or so, the Irish nationalistic movements added a special color to the American scene. They were popular movements designed for the common folk and not for intellectuals; they were not characterized by the presence of lay intellectuals, let alone scholars; they were not intended to promote any of the major ideological movements of the century. Yet, with a great skill they managed to maintain Irish nationalism in America and give considerable weight to the political aims of the home country. By this act they set a pattern that was soon followed by many, and perhaps by all possible, ethnic groups in America. The Poles and Germans in the United States were from the 1830's onward preoccupied with the unification of their homelands and with the pursuit of nationalistic aims centering around their countries of origin. They were followed by the Italians whose national hero, Giuseppe Garibaldi, lived in the United States between 1850 and 1854, earning his living as a candlemaker on Staten Island and giving up his newly established home to lead the military expedition of the Redshirts for the liberation of the Sicilies. As time passed, the smaller nations also joined the nationalistic movement, and Americans of diverse origins—Hungarians, Czechs, Finns, Albanians, Lithuanians, Macedonians, Armenians, Jews—built up their organizations for the political support of their home country.

The nationalism, pursued by the ethnic groups in America, cannot be conceived without an emotional attachment to the old country which served as its natural psychological background. As a political movement, however, it followed very practical goals to which any doctrinal aims became subordinated; it centered around rendering tangible help—material aid as well as political pressure exerted in the United States—to the old country in its political relations. As long as the old country's aim was political independence or fight against an autocratic government, it could command American support without creating any problem; but once independence was achieved, the old country was likely to be involved in territorial claims against a neighboring state and to demand from its sons living in America a loyal support of all such claims. For example, the accomplishment of German unification was immediately followed by German territorial claims for Polish and Baltic provinces in Europe, for colonies in Africa, and, generally, for the imperialistic aims of Grand Admiral Tirpitz.

The ethnic groups in America proved to be rather sensitive to the political suggestions coming from the old country and, as a result, they worked at cross-purposes much the same way as the nations of Europe did. The political goals of the Polish-Americans could hardly be reconciled with those of the Germans, the goals of the Czechoslovaks were opposed to those of the Hungarians and, at present, the Jewish aims for an independent Israel seem to be similarly posed against the political aims of the Arabs. Yet, American public opinion gave sympathy to all these groups and equally endorsed the idea of the Irish, Greek, or Czechoslovak independence. In fact, ethnic nationalism was respectable in itself and made America overlook the fact that aid given to one group would have logically precluded support to another group. Hence, old-country-centered political activity became a regular program for most ethnic groups in which the common-folk immigrant eagerly participated. Any success in achieving those political aims has greatly contributed to the social status of the ethnic group; and even without conspicuous success, old-country nationalism has become a source of respectability that has met with the public approval of the Anglo-Saxon majority and has bestowed personal prestige upon ethnic Americans.

The rise of this hyphenated allegiance did not mean that the pattern of thinking established in John Adams' time was abandoned. The Anglo-Saxon majority tended to reprove those political movements of the immigrants which were directed toward America, toward promoting changes in this country and, particularly, toward propagating radical ideas among Americans. While the nationalistic immigrant organizations usually succeeded in enlisting the support of the homeland as well as of the American public, the émigré of radical leanings had to face animosity from both directions. If he took up his case publicly, he found himself in a rather hopeless predicament and had to make his choice: either to defy almost the whole world or make a compromise with his ideas. The German Forty-eighters, an unusual group of men of ideas, are a case in point. Their history begins with the collapse of the short-lived German revolution of 1848 which sent those many liberals who had been involved in the revolutionary events scurrying from the country. A number of them, and 4,000 is said to be a conservative estimate, eventually landed in America, representing a mass of well-educated immigrants, political thinkers and refugees dedicated to ideas. Their fate after immigration foreshadowed the problems of similar groups arriving in the subsequent decades.

Highly qualified as the Forty-eighters were, upon their arrival in America many of them encountered serious difficulties in finding suitable work and had to take up jobs as cigar makers, waiters, house servants, bootblacks or street sweepers. Associated with this occupational maladjustment was a tendency among them to look upon themselves as exiles who would use the United States simply as a base for promoting a German cause. In this effort they wanted to win, first of all, the co-operation of their compatriots in America with whom they were united in a sentimental attachment to the homeland but not in political aims. Thus, they turned their interest and activity toward the German group, but, in spite of persistent efforts for organizing it, they had to realize their inability to find many German-American followers. The Forty-eighters did not represent the mentality of the common-folk German immigrants who were apathetic to public affairs and disinterested in liberal American causes such as the abolition of slavery. As an especially important point, the German Catholics never ceased to express their animosity toward the anti-clericalism and freethinking of the Forty-eighters, and the two branches of the German-American group proceeded on separate paths.

The Forty-eighters, failures as they were in occupational success or in efforts to unite their compatriots, achieved fame in American history because of their political activities. They were liberals, which meant opposition to the autocratic systems existing in Germany but did not mean a unity of principles or program; in fact, they were sharply divided among themselves, showing a broad range of political shadings. On the radical wing of this political spectrum stood a small group of Communist Forty-eighters like Wilhelm Weitling who endorsed a social revolution and the formation of an American "republic of the workers." A more moderate view was expressed in the Louisville platform of 1854, although it received much publicity as an example of German radicalism. It was the work of such refugees as Karl Heinzen and Bernhard Domschke, and it aimed for the abolition of slavery, the enfranchisement of Negroes and women, social legislation, and (features particularly repulsive to the American public opinion) the abolition of the Senate and Presidency, to be replaced by a unicameral Congress elected by popular vote.

Such political activities evoked a great deal of criticism which often ended in describing the immigrant as a corrupting influence upon the American political life. This accusation, formerly leveled against the French and the Irish but now directed against the Germans, gained a wide acceptance because the German Forty-eighters did carry out a systematic agitation for social-revolutionary aims and attempted to disseminate their ideas among the Anglo-Saxon majority of the country. The reaction to such efforts was understandable. As one historian put it, "the impact of the Forty-eighters kept nativism from dying out completely. Even among Americans with no nativistic inclinations the Forty-eighters were an unpopular group because of their agnosticism and rationalism, their unconcealed contempt for

American culture, and their criticism of such social customs as the Puritan Sabbath." As the Forty-eighters became more involved in organizational work for social and political reforms, "American reaction became palpably sharper. Resentment of German arrogance gave way to excited warnings against the machinations of a disaffected and turbulent element to whom Americans had unwisely given asylum."[2]

Yet, one has to ask how sincere and how widespread radicalism was among the Forty-eighters, many of whom (perhaps the majority, but by all means the most successful segment) ended their public career within the respectable framework of American political institutions. Many of them played a prominent role in the rise of the Republican Party and, from the time of Lincoln on, rendered useful services to the administration. Carl Schurz is perhaps the best known representative of this type who hesitated between the careers of politics and scholarship, and when he finally selected politics, he became remarkably successful in it, rising to become senator from Missouri, Secretary of the Interior, and editor of the New York *Evening Post*. Many others followed this career pattern on a less spectacular scale and received appointments from Lincoln and his successors to the civil service. From 1860 on, a long list of Forty-eighters served in the diplomatic and consular service of the United States: Schurz himself as minister to Spain, Friedrich Haussarek as minister to Ecuador, Theodore Canisius as consul to Vienna and other cities, Hermann Kiefer as consul to Stettin, etc.

In fact, one has to sense a certain ambiguity in the careers of the Forty-eighters, some kind of hesitation between radicalism and respectability which very often was resolved by giving up the imported radicalism and in time assuming American respectability. Rather few Forty-eighters remained lifelong radicals, and many of them passed into the status of prestige—*Ansehen* as they were wont to refer to it in their private correspondence. This ambiguity takes an interesting generational pattern in the case of the Lieber family, father and son, who have written a colorful chapter into the history of American political refugees. Francis Lieber, the father, came to America in the 1820's, served

---

[2] Maldwyn Allen Jones, *American Immigration* (Chicago: University of Chicago Press, 1960), p. 154.

for many years as professor of history and political economy at the University of South Carolina and Columbia University, and as a lifelong liberal and anti-slavery man, he rendered useful services to the Lincoln administration. His son, Oscar Montgomery Lieber, returned to Germany as a young man to study, took part in the street fights of Berlin in March, 1848, and qualified to be counted as a Forty-eighter. Upon his return to America, he settled down to scholarly life in South Carolina. He joined Wade Hampton's legion in the Civil War and in the battle of Williamsburg gave his life for the cause of slavery.

Whether it was due to the lure of respectability or to the natural change of political principles, radicalism slowly abated, and perhaps disappeared, among the Forty-eighters. Their public role ended, strangely enough, with a congratulatory message sent to their old persecutor, King William I of Prussia, upon his defeat of France and assumption of the title of German Emperor.

Just at the time when the Forty-eighters seemed to relinquish their old doctrines for the Kaiser's Germany, European radicalism became revitalized through the example of the Paris Commune. The Communards, to be sure, did not mark a turning point in the history of radicalism, yet they instilled enthusiasm into those who were inclined toward radicalism and horror into those who were opposed to it. The years that followed their fight and downfall witnessed a growth of both pro- and anti-radical sentiments in the countries of the Western world. What happened in America between the financial panic of 1873 and the Sacco-Vanzetti case of the 1920's was but a part of an international phenomenon—the growth and decline of one extremist movement—although American radicalism, at least in its early stage, would have been impossible without the leadership of immigrant intellectuals.

The revolutionary and radical movements which existed during this period had a large and conspicuous foreign-born membership. It was significant that out of the seventeen Socialist newspapers published in the United States in 1876, ten were German, three Bohemian, and one Swedish. The Socialist Labor Party, founded in 1878, was composed largely of immigrants, and, in addition to the Germans, Bohemians and Swedes, the Jews, Finns, and various Slavic groups formed large clusters within its membership. So it was with the anarchist movement which took root in Chicago in the 1880's and, later on, with the Communist parties.

Socialism could not be equated with radicalism, perhaps not even on the American scene where the groupings of political parties and labor movements followed a more conservative line than in many countries of Europe. But the socialist movement in America was a fairly large and stable cadre from which smaller and more radical groups would split off. In 1880, for example, the revolutionary wing left the Socialist Party and joined forces with the anarchist groups animated by Bakunin's ideas. The result was the establishment of the International Working Men's Association for the promotion of anarchism. By 1885 the Association comprised 80 sections with some 8,000 members and produced two German and three English newspapers. Then came the Haymarket Riot in Chicago arousing indignation and hysteria from the part of the public and stern measures from the part of the authorities; with that the back of the anarchist movement was broken.

A few immigrant intellectuals caught the attention of the American public as exponents of radicalism. Among them, John Most, a refugee from Germany and England, became the most dynamic exponent of Bakuninism. His provocative and sarcastic editorials in his German-language weekly appealed to the readers more effectively than any other writings of the extremist press. He preached the "propaganda of the deed" as the surest way of achieving social revolution, and as a practical instruction he published a pamphlet with the self-explanatory title of *Science of Revolutionary Warfare: A Manual of Instructions in the Use and Preparation of Nitro-glycerin, Dynamite, Guncotton, Fulminating Mercury, Bombs, Fuses, Poisons, etc., etc.* Quite understandably, such a revolutionary cookbook made the respectable citizenry shudder. His disciple in English elocution, the Russian-born Emma Goldman, represented not only the feminine mystique but also persistence in radicalism; although her principles and affiliations did change among the many radical movements, she never followed the example of the Forty-eighters in relinquishing radicalism for some more respectable doctrine.

America cannot be accused of xenophobia; her image as a refuge for the oppressed and her belief in the immigrant as a vital factor in the national development have accompanied her history from revolutionary times on. But by the 1880's many Americans "saw the immigrant as a potential assassin and social revolutionary, a competitor for jobs in the East and land in the West, and a general threat to the established institutions and prosperity."[3] The demand for restricting immigration became popular, and the law of 1894 barred the entry of foreign-born anarchists.

The law was a rather crude expression of a lingering national sentiment or rather suspicion against the immigrant intellectual. The following decades, which saw the Industrial Workers of the World and some other movements operating under the leadership of native-born radicals, could not dispel, but only refine, the suspicion that the intellectual who slipped into the country amidst the many immigrants of the laboring class, came not as an honest toiler in the national industry but as a harbinger of subversion. This deep-seated suspicion had a great part in formulating American immigration policy after World War I and in the 1930's, in delaying the admission of those many intellectuals who suffered persecution in Hitler's Germany.

This suspicion, so often voiced in the press and political oratory as well as studies of scholarly pretension, usually overlooked those social conditions in Europe that determined the affiliation of the political refugees coming to America. Up to the end of World War I the autocratic systems that ruled Germany, Russia, and a few other countries of Europe operated in a way that many intellectuals in those countries came to regard socialism or radicalism as the only possible form of protest against the gross iniquities of the existing political regime. Hence, the autocratic countries furnished an inexhaustible reservoir of refugees, many of whom eventually landed in America and caught the public eye. The American publicity given to their newsworthy activities overshadowed the fact that at the same time émigrés representing the more respectable political movements also found their way to America; they were, as a rule, the spokesmen of national

[3] F. C. Jaher, *Doubters and Dissenters* (Glencoe, Ill.: Free Press, 1964), p. 48.

minorities in Eastern Europe. These émigrés prepared on American soil the post-war independence of Czechoslovakia and Poland; among them Tomas Masaryk, Czechoslovak scholar, statesman, and humanist, is perhaps the best-known name.

As the great war ended, many leaders of the national minorities returned home, but, like people moving through a revolving door, new groups of émigrés entered America: Russian refugees of various shades, Hungarian democratic politicians (among them, political scientist Oscar Jaszi) fleeing from the terror of the Horthy regime, opponents of some smaller and often short-lived dictatorships in Europe, the German democratic opposition to Hitler, and also some members of the Spanish democratic opposition to Franco. This was the time when émigrés of all possible doctrinal leanings were active in the United States: old-time radicals as well as monarchists from a country which had changed to republic, spokesmen of the various socialist as well as conservative parties, Fascist as well as pro-Communist exiles. The factions, divided by doctrines, personalities, and ethnic loyalties, were numerous beyond count. They waged an incessant warfare among themselves although the practical exigencies of life often forced upon them a rather strange accommodation, inimical factions using, perhaps in the course of one night, the same lecture hall or the same printing press located in an ethnic neighborhood of our cities.

Amidst this warfare, however, a general shift could be observed in the alignment of the main doctrinal groups. The nationalistic movements appeared to increase in popularity, attracting a greater proportion of adherents in the ethnic population and assuming organized forms in more ethnic groups. On the other hand, the old nineteenth-century radicalism was on the wane, being reduced by the natural attrition of political movements; its adherents were decimated by aging and death, and there was no youth to take their places. The younger generation, if radically inclined, tended to join the new forms of radicalism, the Communist and Fascist movements. The two movements represented a considerable strength on the national scene of the 1930's; both attracted immigrants but, as a matter of policy, tried to operate under native-born leadership and publicly underrate their ethnic support.

The momentous changes that followed World War II, particularly America's clear position in the face of Communism, brought forth a fundamental shift in émigré organizations and principles. The essence of the shift was a great reduction, and even disappearance, of radical movements sponsored by émigrés or backed by ethnic people. If nothing else, then, the general economic boom that the whole Western world has experienced since the end of the war deprived these movements of their best arguments and of their chance to attract young recruits. Out of the ideas that had created so much commotion in the last century, anarchism, disappeared for good; and old-type socialism, incapable of attracting the American-born descendants of immigrants, was greatly weakened. Communism, too, suffered under the forces of erosion; many émigré Communists became disillusioned, while others left America for one of those home countries where Communism had been established at the end of the war. Fascism and Nazism had always been motivated by opportunism and, as soon as their propagation no longer seemed opportune, their adherents tended to drift away and endorse less extremist political ideas.

As another part of the momentous changes, World War II hardly ended when anti-Communist refugees began to arrive and, with the generous support of American public opinion and civic life, initiated large-scale propaganda and organizational work among their compatriots. By 1949 there were not less than ten committees of iron-curtain exiles functioning in the United States, functioning as unofficial governments anxious to liberate their homelands. Their activities, rather well known to the public, are difficult to summarize because they have been surrounded by so much emotionalism and internecine troubles.

Significant of nearly all of the governments-in-exile is that they have been unable to induce their compatriots in America to acknowledge their leadership. There is abundant testimony to the fact that these compatriots, whatever country they come from, are almost without exception loyal to the United States; towards the old country, however, they have not been able to rid themselves of those suspicions, distrusts, doubts, and fears that are rooted in old wrongs and iniquities suffered there. They are unable to establish among themselves a unity of principles and organizations, and they perpetuate the old divisions, especially when the problems of leadership and distribution of power are involved. Since second- and third-generation people of East European origin are quite willing to take up the political problems of the Old World, the often bitter arguments or power struggles do not show signs of reaching an end.

An example is furnished by the difficulties confronting the American Czechs and Slovaks in judging the political aspects of pre-Communist Czechoslovakia. Their problem, in brief, is that in Czechoslovakia there existed an "autonomist" political group which claimed that the Slovaks were an independent nation although their independence was not recognized by the government of Masaryk and Benes. This autonomist theme is enthusiastically endorsed by a Slovak group in America made up of refugees as well as second- and third-generation intellectuals. The academic expression of their ideology can be found in several publications; one of them, written by a "member of the Slovak Institute" and professor at an accredited university in America, argues as follows:

> The peoples of the Western world generally know little about Slovakia, and the little that they know is unfortunately laden with errors. . . . It was Magyar "political science" which first tried to put the resources of erudition into the service of politics. . . . Between the two wars, Czech "political science" ensured relief. Conceiving an alleged unity of language and culture, it invented the myth of a "Czechoslovak" nationality. Czech historians and linguists attempted to dissolve Slovak individuality in an artificial community and furnish arguments to the politicians responsible for the new state: Masaryk and Benes. The "political science" of the Western nations fell into step. Instead of going to the sources, as would have been proper, it preferred to take the easy way and utilize Czech and Magyar works. . . . It goes without saying—so natural it is—that each time a patriotic act was evidenced in Slovakia, instead of seeking its really deep causes, the government preferred to attribute a foreign origin to it, thereby justifying the most bloody repressions.[4]

[4] Joseph A. Mikus, *Slovakia* (Milwaukee: Marquette University Press, 1963), pp. xv-xviii.

The petulant tone of the text, which suggests that Slovak political science is the only political science worthy of being named without quotation marks of pejorative connotation, is characteristic of quite a few authors of diverse national backgrounds. Many of these authors claim to have suffered under the political conditions in their homelands and have developed scholarly interests in order to be able to continue their political activities in America. In this way a great many academically trained refugees continue to work against the political system which had driven them into exile and for the political cause which they had been supporting in the old country. The Slovak separatist movement is not the only case of its kind; it is paralleled by a similar Croatian movement centered around the "Dominican House of Studies (For Croatian Culture)" and directed by a physician, and by another movement aimed for "independent Macedonia." Perhaps it is not entirely frivolous to include among the fighters for dead issues the International Peasant Union, organized in Washington for a cause which has no meaning in America—a country which never had a peasant class—and has hardly any future in Europe where peasantry is more or less extinct; its restoration as a part of a semi-feudal class structure does not appear to be imminent.

The questions of leadership which plague all such refugee movements pose a more difficult problem which, as history suggests, cannot be solved. The émigré movements, as so many examples prove, do not become more unified but more divided with the passing of time; the years spent in exile increase rather than reduce the factions. Their never-ending dissensions are lengthily, and often passionately, discussed in the foreign-language press; however, they come to the attention of the American public only on such rather rare occasions when they develop into chronic troubles (as the case is with the Cuban refugees since Castro's revolution) or result in violence. American public opinion evidently was in sympathy with such incidents as the picket lines of protesting Serbians, Croatians, and Slovenians at the time of Marshal Tito's visit to the United States. Similarly, the American press paid great attention, although less sympathy, to the bitter division that developed among members of the Serbian Orthodox Church in the United States and Canada over the church ties with the Holy Synod in Yugoslavia, a division that led to violence and police interference in the Serbian Orthodox churches of Cleveland and Chicago. To mention an old but still-remembered case, American public opinion was greatly aroused when Archbishop Leon Tourian of the Armenian Church in America was assassinated by the Armenian Revolutionary Federation on the morning of Christmas Sunday, 1933, as he was about to celebrate Mass in his church in New York City.

The present-day émigrés, to be sure, are not here to shock America. As they assure us in so many announcements, they prefer to use dignified means for achieving respectable goals. One may rightly ask: What is the criterion of respectability in political actions, and particularly in émigré politics, where each group follows its own purposes and the idea of civic co-operation is of no great concern? It is evident that respectability comes not so much from the unity of action or from the content of political doctrines that any refugee group manifests, but from the sympathetic approval given to the group by American public opinion, or rather by the leaders of our system of mass communication. After all, no citizen can honestly scrutinize the doctrines of numberless political organizations that are presented in a highly rhetorical form and often in a foreign language; this scrutiny must be made either on the basis of special knowledge or, if it is made by the average citizen, must be based on superficial manifest actions that reach the publicity of newspapers.

In this sense there are at present rather few and small radical groups of émigrés, and the most conspicuous of them, the pro-Castro movement is, while disapproved by the Americans, extenuatingly ascribed to the mercurial temperament of Latin-American politics. On the other hand, the numerous anti-Communist émigré organizations are heartily approved by the media of public opinion because they seem to work for political goals highly respected in America. Participation in such movements is a matter of personal respectability much the same way as activity in any civic group is, and a great many American-born citizens of ethnic origin participate in them.

No doubt about it, our generation has witnessed the decline of foreign-born radicalism in this country, and there are some good reasons which account for this fact. The anarcho-syndicalist and Communist movements of the immigrants could flourish in America as long as there was no governmental or civic agency which could have dealt systematically with the problem of radicalism. But over the last few decades a network of such agencies has been built up which can, and does, effectively check the disapproved movements. At present, the John Mosts and Alexander Berkmans would not be able to take up their organizational activities in Chicago or New York while the network of civic and governmental agencies efficiently encourages all the respectable political organizations of émigré leadership.

The radical movements of the last century were independent and self-contained, while the present-day respectable émigré organizations are likely to work in co-operation with the civic and governmental agencies of America. Such a situation raises questions: What should be the limit of this co-operation? At what point should agitation on behalf of causes not in line with American politics be stopped? The problem underlying the public control of refugee politics can be put in general terms: How far does the right of the foreign-born citizen in America extend to carry out organized political activities on behalf of his native country? Seeing the perennial conflicts within and among the émigré organizations, one is tempted to add one more question: How far is the immigrant entitled to thrash out in the new country the bitter controversies and personal animosities of old-country politics and transmit their continuation to his children and other Americans?

Such questions are seldom asked in public and then they are usually dismissed with a reference to our cultural pluralism. This kind of response tacitly assumes that culture and politics are identical—for example, that teaching Spanish at one of our universities is an activity of the same order as carrying out agitation for or against the Franco system. In another context I attempted to delineate the political limits of cultural pluralism, and at present I would like to note only one idea. The moral and legal limitations that the self-interest of America has to place upon the homeland-centered political activities of émigrés and ethnic groups—a problem that has been a taboo for all too long—needs to be publicly discussed and clarified. Otherwise, we shall persist in the present not altogether satisfactory situation where any organized group, which is powerful in membership or means, can exert an undue influence upon American politics and impose political obligations upon the country that are not necessarily in the best interest of the majority of the citizens.

The discussion of this problem is desirable, but I have no great hopes that it would take place in the near future. The popular émigré movements of the present time are so respectable that they try to avoid anything that might be controversial, while the radical movements which are likely to arouse the concern of the average American are well under control. In view of this situation, one might attempt to assess the total impact of the foreign-born radical upon the American scene. Since his impact has never resulted in appreciable, let alone violent, changes of our political system, the problem should be formulated in more academic terms: What was the influence of the foreign-born radical upon American mentality and, particularly, political philsophy?

These foreign-born radicals, to be sure, set to work in America with the notion of realizing here their doctrinaire plans; but, intellectuals and erudite minds as many of them were, they set to work with a basic ignorance of those social forces that prevail in this country. They planned their work as a straight continuation of activities begun in the old country and they acted as if they were fighting German or Russian autocracy in Washington, New York, or Chicago. Consequently, they had an appeal to their countrymen with similar experiences and sentiments; but they were working for themselves, their own group, and homeland; they were, even in their general transformation from radicalism to respectability, outside the mainstream of American life. It happened only temporarily and under very special circumstances, such as a depression, that they were able to reach out toward the non-ethnic American, and even then they reached but a few. Through their activities they added something to the American flexibility in political thinking, but they never converted the majority of Americans, never taught them ideas of lasting impact. Their own ideas never became fertile seeds out of which new plants, or perhaps weeds, would have grown. The history of the émigrés, even with its present respectable period, makes interesting reading, but it is an item of curiosity and not an essential chapter in American history.

JULIUS REZLER

The Scholar as Policy Maker

WE HAVE A MENTAL PICTURE of the immigrant as an outsider or stranger who somewhat timidly progresses toward becoming assimilated into the culture of his new homeland. The picture represents him as an apolitical man, unready and unqualified to play a role in the public life of his new country and not expected to do so. What he is expected to do after his arrival is to mobilize all his energies for establishing and adjusting himself in the new culture. Only after making a place for himself in the new economy and getting acquainted with the new environment is he supposed to consider some political activity, probably in the local area and perhaps within his own group.

This image, still common among us, evidently refers to the past. Speaking of former decades, a sharp observer of the American scene concluded, "Even had the immigrants been inclined to political activity, they would have found it difficult. At first, their rising generation found little real identification with either of the major parties. In exchange for a favor or a two-dollar bill the newly naturalized worker would vote the way the political machine instructed."[1]

Recent events in American politics, however, demand that this old conception of the immigrant be sharply revised. Since the time of World War II quite a few immigrant scholars have exerted a profound influence on the national policy of the United States, and may, indeed, have changed the course of American history. These scholars became involved in politics almost as soon as they landed; their activities were greatly encouraged by native political leaders; and they made their contribution, whatever it was, on an individual basis. They differed in almost every respect from the old type of immigrant.

[1] Samuel Lubell, *The Future of American Politics* (New York: Harper, 1951), p. 37.

113

In the 1930's, due to the political upheavals in the countries of Central and Southeast Europe, the social composition of the immigrants changed radically. As a consequence of political and religious persecution by Fascism, Nazism, and Communism, a great number of scholars, teachers, and other professionals left their native countries to escape the suppression of their cherished ideas or to avoid persecution. They arrived in the United States in three major waves. The first wave consisted of those fleeing Hitler's Germany and the countries overrun by the Nazi army. The second wave, much larger in numbers, arrived after the conclusion of World War II. It brought to this country survivors of the Nazi concentration camps, sons of the Southeast European countries now occupied by the Soviet army, and, as the most homogeneous group, more than a hundred German missile experts, who late in 1945 were transferred to the first rocket research center at Fort Bliss, Texas. The third wave of immigrant scholars came from Hungary after the Soviet suppression of the Hungarian revolution in 1956.

Only scanty data are available on the number of scholars coming to the United States. According to the records of the Immigration and Naturalization Service, 11,000 natural scientists were admitted to the United States from all parts of the world in the years between 1949 and 1961.[2] To this figure, however, one has to add the unknown number of the representatives of other disciplines such as humanities, arts, and social and political sciences—a number that might be several times larger than the previously mentioned one.

Representatives of two disciplines—natural sciences, particularly physics and chemistry, and political science—were mainly called upon to participate in American politics. Their involvement in politics can be explained by the existence of the national needs created by World War II and the Cold War, needs that these scholars, by their talent and previous experience, were not only eminently suited, but also ready and willing, to satisfy.

Foremost of those needs was the development of a revolutionary weapons system without which the United States could not

[2] U.S. National Science Foundation, *Scientific Manpower from Abroad* (Washington, D.C., 1962).

have preserved its independence, freedom, and status as a world power against the aggressively expanding Soviet Union. Ever since the first years of World War II, immigrant physicists and chemists, primarily because of their dedication to basic research, have been playing a decisive role in the development of the major weapon systems, the mainstay of American defense. It was the good fortune of the United States that, in time of national emergency, the talents and knowledge of such leading European scientists as the German-born Einstein and Bethe, the Hungarian-born Teller, Szilard, Wigner and von Neuman, the Italian Fermi, and the Danish Bohr became available to this country.

The immigrant political scientists were called upon to satisfy another national need, the formulation of new concepts for a successful foreign policy in the Cold War. Up to this time there had been a remarkable lack of long-term concepts in American foreign and defense policy. For the greater part of its history, America had been separated from the other parts of the world partly by the oceans and partly by the traditional attitude of isolationism which viewed any intervention in foreign affairs as a temporary evil. As the events during and after World War I aptly illustrate, the United States, after solving a particular problem of international policy, always retreated to its splendid isolation.

Henry Kissinger, an astute analyst of foreign policy in the nuclear age, has pointed out that certain features of the American psyche were responsible for this situation. "Foremost among the attitudes which affect the making of our policy," he reasoned, "is American empiricism and its quest for certainty. . . . Empiricism in foreign policy leads to a penchant for *ad hoc* solutions. The rejection of dogmatism inclines our policy-makers to postpone committing themselves until all facts are in; but by the time the facts are in, a crisis has usually developed or an opportunity has passed. Our policy is, therefore, geared to dealing with emergencies; it finds difficulty in developing the long-range program that might forestall them." The lack of a "tragic experience" is another factor in the apparent difficulty of the United States in formulating foreign-policy concepts. "The American domestic experience exhibits an unparalleled success. . . . It is no wonder, therefore, that to many of our most responsible men the warnings of impending peril or of imminent disaster sound like the Cassandra cries of abstracted 'eggheads.' "[3]

For such reasons it has become the task of immigrant political scientists to make up for certain deficiencies in their American colleagues and to assist them in developing political strategies for the Cold War, a task for which they were well qualified by their background and experience. They came from Europe, the scene of power politics for centuries, and the study of the intricate power relations of the European states enabled them to offer a frame of reference which could be applied to the American situation.

The emergence of the Soviet Union as a world power created further need for political scientists intimately familiar with the Soviet scene. Up to the late 1950's, only a limited number of native-born American political scientists understood the Russian language sufficiently to permit them to study the primary sources of information concerning Communist society, and hardly anybody had had the opportunity for an on-the-scene observation of Soviet countries. The vacuum created by the lack of American experts was filled by immigrant scholars who were born in Russia or had lived under Soviet rule. In the first decade of the Cold War the American government in formulating its strategy relied on the knowledge furnished by the foreign-born Soviet experts such as Alexander Erlich, Gregory Grossman, Naum Jasny, Lazar Volin. Naturally it was unavoidable that, in the course of evaluating Soviet policies and conditions, the immigrant experts would inadvertently influence American policy makers by their own value judgments and attitudes toward the Soviet regime.

As the attention of the American foreign-policy makers has increasingly turned toward Communist China, a new group of immigrant political scientists were called upon to interpret the political and economic manifestations of this growing power and to offer new proposals for formulating a workable foreign policy vis-à-vis Red China. The Yugoslav-born Alexander Eckstein and the Chinese-born Tang-Tsou, Chin-yuan Cheng, Nai-Ruenn Chen, to name only a few, are among the "China

[3] Henry A. Kissinger, *Nuclear Weapons and Foreign Policy* (New York: Harper, 1957), pp. 424, 426.

watchers" frequently invited by congressional committees and academic symposia.

The national needs, as they emerged, required important contributions from immigrant scholars. Should it be taken for granted that these scholars were under obligation to render whatever services were requested of them? Most of them felt definitely obliged to co-operate with American authorities, but their extraordinary efforts, especially on the part of the atomic physicists, were primarily due to their identification with the United States. They were not only grateful for the hospitality and opportunities received, but they also accepted, to a great extent, the values of American society, notably those of freedom and democracy. They also were motivated by their desire to develop science, learn its secrets, and extend the boundaries of knowledge. As Edward Teller put it, "The duty of scientists is to explore and explain. Thus duty led to the invention of the principles that made the hydrogen bomb a practical reality."[4] The overwhelming desire to explore the unknown may explain the apparent contradiction that atomic physicists with pacifist principles did participate in the development of the A-bomb.

Besides the call of duty, the immigrant scientists were led by other motives, such as their desire to "get even" with the oppressive regimes that had forced them to leave their former countries. This was one of the reasons for Einstein and Szilard writing their famous letter to President Roosevelt about the necessity of producing the A-bomb. The political scientists from Southeast Europe were also eager to promote the liberation of their native countries from Soviet domination.

The concrete contributions by which immigrant scholars directly or indirectly influenced American policy and public opinion can be conveniently classified into three categories: the physical development of new weapons systems; the advancement of principles concerning the acceptance, use, and testing of these systems; and, finally, the formulation of new concepts for American strategy in the Cold War.

The most important single contribution to American security

[4] Edward Teller (with Allen Brown), *The Legacy of Hiroshima* (New York: Doubleday, 1962), p. 56.

and survival that the immigrant scientists have made is their participation in the development of the three major weapons systems: the A-bomb, the H-bomb, and the various missiles. In the initial phase of developing the A-bomb, the basic scientific principles for future production were established by Fermi, Bohr, Szilard, Rabi, and others. The solution of the technical problems which stood in the way of the production of the H-bombs were largely solved by Edward Teller. A group of German scientists should be credited with the experimental development of American rockets and missiles.

Immigrant scientists did not, however, limit themselves to purely technical laboratory problems. They exerted a powerful influence on national policy decisions in connection with the acceptance, use, and testing of these weapons. In July, 1939, when the clouds of World War II were already gathering, Leo Szilard and Eugen Wigner visited Albert Einstein at his summer house. Szilard and Wigner, who at that time were physicists unknown outside the scientific community, recognized the potentials of the ongoing laboratory experiments which eventually led to the splitting of the atom and knew that those potentials could lead to developments which would affect the national security. At their urging, Einstein somewhat reluctantly informed President Roosevelt in a letter that "it may become possible to set up a nuclear chain reaction in a large mass of uranium, by which vast amounts of power would be generated. Now it appears almost certain that this could be achieved in the immediate future. This new phenomenon would also lead to the construction of bombs, and it is conceivable that extremely powerful bombs of a new type may thus be constructed."[5]

Einstein had no more part in the development of the A-bomb, and later, as we are told, he was sorry even for the small role he had played. At a Nobel Prize anniversary dinner in December, 1945, he revealed some of his feelings on the matter: "Today, the physicists who participated in forging the most formidable and dangerous weapon of all times are harassed by an equal feeling of responsibility."[6]

[5] E. Teller, *The Legacy of Hiroshima*, pp. 10-11.
[6] Peter Michelmore, *Einstein: Profile of the Man* (New York: Dodd, Mead, 1962), pp. 233-34.

Soon afterward, Edward Teller carried the fight for another favorable government decision of developing and producing the hydrogen bomb. In 1949 the report of the General Advisory Committee of the Atomic Commission stated: "We all hope that by one means or another, the development of these weapons can be avoided." It was a unanimous statement reflecting the opinion of Robert Oppenheimer, the chairman of the committee. But Teller strongly felt that "the Russians would follow their development of a fission bomb with a success in fusion," and turned to Senator McMahon, chairman of the Atomic Energy Committee of the Congress, urging him that "it is vital to the nation's defense that we proceed with the thermo-nuclear work."[7] After the intervention of McMahon and Lewis Strauss, President Truman overrode the negative recommendation of the Advisory Committee and ordered the development of the H-bomb. For this political-scientific role, Teller was rightly named the "Father of the H-bomb."

Once the nuclear bombs were developed and the scientists realized the true consequence of their work, they felt a strong responsibility for their "brain-child" and did not hesitate to take a firm stand whenever a political controversy developed over the use and testing of nuclear weapons.

The first argument over the use of the A-bomb developed near the end of World War II. Szilard took a firm stand against its use in the Japanese war. He drafted a petition, which was subsequently signed by seventy of his fellow scientists involved in the Manhattan Project, advising President Truman not to use the bomb "unless the terms which will be imposed upon Japan have been made public in detail and Japan knowing these terms, refused to surrender."[8] The petition never reached Truman, whose decision to drop the bomb over Hiroshima was supported by Enrico Fermi, another immigrant scientist.

To test or not to test has become another controversial question of national policy in which immigrant scholars have been playing a major role. It has been a cornerstone of American foreign policy to seek a treaty limiting the testing of nuclear de-

---

[7] E. Teller, *The Legacy of Hiroshima*, pp. 42-44.

[8] Fletcher Knebel and C. W. Bailey, "The Fight over the A-Bomb," *Look*, August 13, 1963, p. 22.

vices, assuming that such a test ban could be politically and scientifically controlled. Particularly, much attention has been paid to scientific methods of policing a prospective test ban, and therefore, governmental and congressional authorities have solicited with increasing frequency the expert opinion of scientists. Despite the large number of scientists participating in the hearings, panels, and symposia dealing with the problem of testing, the voices of two immigrant atom physicists, Hans Bethe and Edward Teller have dominated the discussion; the controversy over testing has become a scientific and political dialogue between the two. Their argument centers around such basic questions as: Are there appropriate and foolproof scientific methods available to police an eventual test moratorium or ban? Would such a test ban treaty not arrest the development of American nuclear weapons and thereby freeze the United States in an inferior position against the Soviet Union? Can the reliability and good intentions of the Soviet Union be assumed?

On the question of policing a test ban agreement, Bethe recommended the acceptance of a system of seismographic stations located in the Soviet Union to detect underground tests. As he stated succinctly, "there are a number, actually a large number, of very good methods to improve the system" of inspection. Teller was adamant in his arguments against the reliability of scientific inspection methods. In his words, "If the Russians want to perform systematic clandestine tests they can do so."[9] The fact that underground testing was excepted from the nuclear test ban treaty signed in July 1963 seems to indicate that the American government accepted Teller's views concerning the undetectability of such tests.

As to the second issue, Bethe was convinced that a test ban treaty would be more advantageous to the United States than to the Soviet Union. He reasoned that "further testing by both sides would bring the Russian capability closer and closer to ours. If we stop nuclear testing now we may keep at least the little bit of military advantage in nuclear weapons that we still

[9] Earl H. Voss, *Nuclear Ambush* (Chicago: Regnery, 1963), p. 151; Hans A. Bethe and Edward Teller, *The Future of Nuclear Tests* (New York: Foreign Relations Association, 1961), p. 53.

possess at the present time." In contrast, Teller strongly advocated the continuation of all types of testing because he believed that "the Russians are developing their war machinery faster than we are. If both of us would stop nuclear testing, then there is no doubt that through espionage they would find out sooner or later what we know, and then we would have lost our last advantage." Accordingly, when concluding his testimony before a congressional committee on the recently signed test ban treaty, Teller emphatically stated, "The treaty is not a step toward peace, but a step away from safety and maybe toward war. It weakens U.S. defenses and invites attack."[10]

On the issue of Soviet reliability, Bethe was convinced that the Russians did not want to violate the test ban treaty: "I believe that they are sincere in wanting the nuclear test cessation agreement and do not intend to cheat on it." Teller, on the other hand, made no secret of his deep distrust of Soviet intentions and spoke up against a treaty which he believed could not be fully controlled: "If we enter into a treaty where the pretense is made that we can be checking, where there are really great loopholes and possibilities of evasion, then I feel that I must raise my voice as a scientist in protest."[11]

The conflicting arguments of Bethe and Teller have been reverberating in the halls of Congress, the offices of the government, the editorial rooms of the newspapers, and all over the country; they have considerably influenced the public opinion of America. The signing of a limited test ban treaty between the United States and the Soviet Union appears to support Bethe's contention, but the negative vote of nineteen U.S. Senators and the uneasy feelings of many Americans over the treaty indicate that Teller's views are shared by a broad segment of the American public.

Political scientists, unlike their colleagues in the field of na-

[10] Bethe and Teller, *The Future of Nuclear Tests*, pp. 34-35; U.S. Senate, A Subcommittee of the Committee on Foreign Relations; *Hearings on Control and Reduction of Armaments*, 85th Congress, 2nd Session, 1958, p. 1463; *U.S. News and World Report*, September 2, 1963, p. 55.

[11] Bethe and Teller, *The Future of Nuclear Tests*, p. 14; Joint Committee on Atomic Energy, *Hearings on Technical Aspects of Detection and Inspection Controls of Nuclear Weapons Test Ban*, 86th Congress, 1960, p. 165.

tural sciences, have not developed revolutionary weapons for the arsenal of the United States. Instead, they have contributed to the defense of this country by creating new ideas, by calling attention to the deteriorating position of the United States in the international arena, by pointing out the major shortcomings of American defense and foreign policy, and by developing concepts for strategies in the Cold War.

The foreign-born political scientists were genuinely appalled by what they regard as the indifference and optimism of the American public in the face of the declining international status of the United States. The Austrian-born Robert Strausz-Hupé and the former Austrian Stefan Possony, in a joint study, remarked: "For several years, the United States and the Free World have steadily lost ground in the international struggle with Communism. If this process continues, it may, within the foreseeable future, become irreversible." Nor could the German-born economist Oscar Morgenstern find more encouragement in the international situation: "Since the end of World War II the position of the United States has steadily deteriorated and is continuing to do so at increased speed."[12]

It is quite possible that these immigrant scholars have reacted to American over-optimism with over-pessimism. But on the basis of their past "tragic experience," they could not help but sense an approaching storm. In any case, they have not stopped by pointing to the dwindling power of the United States, but have also offered some constructive criticisms and suggestions. Strausz-Hupé started out with the proposition: "The U.S. and its allies still lack the weapons, strategies and policies that could cope with fair assurance of success with situations calling for the *measured* use of force." He blamed the "chronic apathy," "neutralist and pacifist tendencies," "psychological disarmament," and "irrational aberration from the traditional purpose of military power," all of which are prevalent tendencies in Western democracies, as being responsible for this situation. He concluded that "America and her associates, their commitments to the cause

[12] Robert Strausz-Hupé, William R. Kintner and Stefan T. Possony (eds.), *A Forward Strategy for America* (New York: Harper, 1961), p. ix; Oscar Morgenstern, *The Question of National Defense* (New York: Random House, 1959), pp. 9-10.

of freedom notwithstanding, have failed to rally their moral and material strength sufficiently to enhance and extend freedom."[13]

His colleagues voiced similar opinions. Morgenstern noted a "distressing confusion" displayed by the American public in politics; Hungarian-born Stephen Kertesz spoke of important structural defects in the foreign-policy machinery of the United States; and Polish-born Zbigniew Brzezinski names the "wild swings of public and press opinion" in reacting to Soviet actions as factors in the unsteady trend of our foreign policy.[14]

The analysis of the United States' deteriorating position in the Cold War and realization of its causes led some immigrant political scientists to the conclusion that new strategies based on novel concepts are needed. The immigrant experts were unanimous in recommending the formulation of a conceptual framework for our actions. German-born Henry Kissinger repeatedly emphasized the need for a doctrine that would establish a response to the most likely challenges. "The nuclear age," he argued, "demands above all a clarification of a doctrine. Strategic doctrine transcends the problem of selecting weapons systems. It is a mode of survival of a society. . . . It is the task of strategic doctrine to translate power into policy."[15]

Strausz-Hupé advocated that the United States should clearly set its strategic goals and "should steer clear of political objectives which it cannot achieve with appropriate military means." The strategy of the Communist bloc, so he and his associates argue, is based on the concept of "protracted conflict," a name coined by Mao Tse-tung in his classical book on Communist warfare: "The strategy of protracted conflict postpones the decisive battle and calibrates its challenges to a calculus of risks—until the balance of power has shifted overwhelmingly to the side of the revolutionary forces." This objective the Communists achieve through "the constant shifting of the battleground, weapons systems and operational tactics for the purpose of confusing the opponent, keeping him off balance and wearing down

[13] R. Strausz-Hupé *et al.*, *A Forward Strategy*, pp. 9, 14, 407-8.

[14] O. Morgenstern, *The Question of National Defense*, p. 4; Stephen D. Kertesz (ed.), *American Diplomacy in a New Era* (Notre Dame, Ind.: University of Notre Dame Press, 1961), p. 10; *U.S. News and World Report*, September 30, 1963, p. 72.

[15] H. A. Kissinger, *Nuclear Weapons and Foreign Policy*, pp. 403, 407.

his resistance." Morgenstern went a step further in drawing up a conceptual framework when he recognized that the Cold War resembles "a game of cold poker between the Kremlin and the administration in Washington" in which "bluffing is indispensable."[16]

One could add many more ideas produced by the fertile mind of immigrant scholars, such as strategic concepts for a hot war (Strausz-Hupé and Possony), mobile weaponry and the establishment of a second striking force (Teller), guerilla warfare (Kissinger), as well as ideas about a greater understanding toward neutralism (Brzezinski) or softening the rigidity of the American policy toward China. But it is, perhaps, unnecessary to point out the great variety of ideas on the theme of the Cold War that the immigrants discussed when there is a question of more practical consequence: What influence did these scholars exert?

Because of the secrecy which necessarily surrounds the strategic plans of the American government in the Cold War, it is difficult to assess in exact terms the impact of the immigrant scholars' ideas and suggestions on American foreign and defense policy. At best, one has to resort to indirect methods to measure that impact. The influence of these scholars can be inferred, however, from the frequency of their official and unofficial utterances, from the number of statements they have made before congressional committees, from their participation in official advisory bodies, from their appearances on radio and television, and from their appearances in print as authors or subjects of books and articles.

The majority of the scientists mentioned here have been, at one time or another, members of governmental committees where, in an operative or consultative capacity, they were in a position to influence the decision-making process of the American government. Enrico Fermi was one of the four members of the Scientific Advisory Panel which in 1945 advised President Roosevelt in the use of the atom bomb. After the war the Gen-

---

[16] R. Strausz-Hupé et al., A Forward Strategy, p. 138; R. Strausz-Hupé et al. (eds.), Protracted Conflict (New York: Harper, 1959), p. 2; O. Morgenstern, "The Cold War is Cold Poker," New York Times Magazine, February 5, 1961.

eral Advisory Committee of the Atomic Energy Commission was the foremost consultative body of the American government in policies concerning atomic weapons and devices. In this eight-member body, Fermi and Rabi served up to the early fifties; then Teller, Szilard, and von Neuman served as members. Hans Bethe was a member of the President's Scientific Advisory Committee during the Eisenhower administration and also acted as member of the U.S. delegation at the Geneva conference on the cessation of nuclear tests.

The immigrant scholars have exerted considerable influence on the members of the Congress in their frequent appearances before congressional committees. For example, Teller and Bethe dominated the hearings of the Joint Committee on Atomic Energy of the Congress dealing in 1958 with the control and reduction of atomic weapons, and in 1960 with the technical aspects of inspection controls of nuclear weapons test ban. The role played by Teller during the hearings of the Senate Preparedness Subcommittee, which examined the possible effects of the nuclear test ban treaty of 1963, was covered in detail by the national press; Teller's opposition to the treaty was endorsed or rejected by hundreds of editorials and by even more letters to the editor. The appearances of the foreign-born political scientists before the Foreign Relations Committee of the Congress were just as numerous, although their contributions might have been more theoretical in nature.

The mass communication media, which control the popularity of those who appeal to public attention, made household words out of the names of some atomic scientists, although one may wonder whether they influenced popularity in due proportion to the scholars' actual contribution to national affairs. Undoubtedly the mass communication media served to convey the ideas of the immigrant scholars to a large segment of the public. As one indication of this, the *Readers' Guide*, which indexes the articles published in some, but not all, leading American magazines, lists approximately 140 articles published between 1945 and 1961 by, or about, the five well-known immigrant atomic physicists. As a consequence of the continuous and sometimes extensive exposure to the views and arguments of immigrant scholars, the public could not help being affected by them. Because of the close interrelationship between American public opinion and government policy, the immigrant scholar, by influencing public opinion, has obtained another means of affecting governmental policy making.

The case of the immigrant scholar in America brings out two interesting points about the operation of historical forces. One point relates to the internal weakness of totalitarian regimes. As the totalitarian governments emerged on the scene of international politics as powerful threats, their very totalitarianism contributed to the erosion of their own power; they forced some of their best brains to leave the country, and to seek refuge and work in the United States. The other point concerns the internal strength of America. The United States has a long-standing tradition of absorbing and integrating immigrants at the social level which corresponds to their education and ability. In the case of the immigrant scholar, she offered a unique opportunity to the newcomers to work in their special fields, to further their professional careers, and, at the same time, to make important contributions to their host country.

While the immigrant scholars' contribution in developing nuclear devices stands out clearly, it is more difficult to evaluate their influence in advancing political concepts. The immigrant atomic physicists have been sharply divided with regard to such important issues as the use, testing, and ban of atomic weapons. It might be contended that as a consequence of their conflicting view, their political influence in promoting one line of action was neutralized; but it is equally true that through their arguments they have helped to clarify the issues and to accelerate the decision-making process in this important area of national policy.

Although the immigrant scholar has worked in an era when both the official policy and public opinion of the United States have fluctuated widely, he has played a complex, articulate, and influential role on the contemporary American scene. In the areas of foreign policy and national defense, his part may even have been crucial. But, with the immigrant scholar being ever active and the national policy ever in a flux, it is better to refrain from evaluating his role. Let us leave it to the judgment of future historians to assign the praise where it duly belongs.

Arms and Visions

An Inquiry into the Feasibility
of Messianism in Our Epoch

ENGLISH NOVELIST C. P. SNOW is a sharp-eyed observer
of men and actions; in fact, many of his characters seem to be
equally indigenous to either side of the ocean. Here is the ambiguity of his latest novel, *Corridors of Power*, which plays
around the Parliament and Whitehall, this inimitably London
setting, unlike anything that does, or may, exist in the District
of Columbia; but it places on this stage a character who im-
presses me with recognizably Washingtonian traits. This character by the name of Dr. Brodzinski (so oddly sounding in the
corridors of Whitehall) happens to be a refugee of the 1930's,
an atomic scientist equally involved in government politics and
weaponry sciences. His policy concerning atomic weapons was
simple enough: "The more the better." And if this axiom became in his hands a principle of international maneuvering, it
was mainly so because Dr. Brodzinski "retained an implacable
confidence throughout, absolutely assured both that he was
right and that he must prevail." His colleagues and rivals, raised
in the traditions of Cambridge and the civil service, regarded
him as a "mad Pole, whose only uncertainty was whether he
hated Russians as Russians more than Russians as Communists."
But if Dr. Brodzinski did not carry his colleagues, he did carry
influential masses because his simple axiom was the message
"what a lot of people wanted to hear." With this appeal he could
blow up a whirlwind of sentiments and, like a cyclone racing
across the plains, play havoc with the regulars of Whitehall who
happened to oppose his policy.

Somehow this fascinating Dr. Brodzinski seems familiar to me. With the usual embarrassment of the *déjà vu*, I have to ask: Did I meet him somewhere before? The time and place elude my memory. It is evident that I recognize an impersonal literary encounter; I must have met the principle and operational method of Brodzinski but not his person. In this way my mind recalls John Kosa's essay contending that success and stand make a scholar. From the point of view of success the genial Pole fills the bill perfectly; he demands, pursues and achieves it in his own non-philistine and non-financial terms. When examining his stand, I am for a moment flabbergasted; but then it occurs to me that one has to enlarge upon the concept of stand to make it fit the case of Brodzinski. I fancy that stand, this essential element in the scholarly personality, comes in two forms, or rather sizes, and gives us two types among the scientists.

When I think of the majority of scholars (and intellectuals as well), I can discern in them a moderately sized inclination to take their stand. It is a reasonable inclination which adapts itself to the circumstances of the given time and space; makes a person discharge the duty of a stand without any detriment to those other duties that every man owes to himself, his family and community; and makes him realize that man's principles are always the outcomes of a constant dialogue with his fellow men. Behold the prudence and cunning of the great scholars: Isaac Newton's religious principles were contrary to the official conformity, John Stuart Mill's liberalism was disapproved by the governors of the East India Company, and John Dewey never recoiled from endorsing causes that outright horrified the educationalists and school-board members. Yet, no harm accrued to their careers because they divided their attention among the many activities of life and their success hinged on their scholarship rather than on their stand.

In the case of other people the stand comes in a tall size, as a dominant feature of the personality, even as a kind of obsession. The principles of such a man do not issue from a dialogue and are not subject to doubts or to a prudent compromise. His principles are hard, his stand unswerving and universal, and he himself seems to be ready to take up a mission upon earth, give his

stand to mankind, and dedicate his career to nothing but messianistic aims.

Is it not a turbulent stream of thoughts that would connect
the name of Dr. Brodzinski with messianism? We live in the age
of physics, affluence, mass society and psychotherapy; we are
prone to regard messianism as something historical and mainly
religious. The books of history tell us of the great men of religion who came to announce a spiritual message, preached it
undaunted by adversities, indifference, and resistance, and exem-
plified it in the deeds, sufferings, and sacrifices of their lives.
But the books of history also show that religious content is not
an indispensable condition of the message; messianism can, and
does, pursue secular aims—the happiness of mankind upon
earth, the removal of social evils, sickness, and ignorance. Verily,
the twofold aims cannot be always separated, and religious as
well as secular missionaries equally reach out for the same goals.
The history of the communitarian settlements in America begins
with immigrants who brought a religious message to this continent, with Mother Ann Lee of the Shakers, Father Rapp of
the Separatists, Christian Metz of the Inspirationists at Amana,
and the Veregin family of the Canadian Dukhobors; but it continues with the secular aims of co-operative socialism announced
by a different set of immigrants, by Robert Owen and his New
Harmony, by Etienne Cabet and his Icarian colonies. There was
no historical break in the influx of messages. The secular missionary often took up work at the point where the religious had
left it off. Owen bought the colony built by Rapp and renamed
it New Harmony; Cabet acquired the place of Nauvoo from the
Mormons who had moved further on their journey to the
promised land; and the Con-Society Family, a native-born scheme
of communitarian living designed by old-stock New Englanders,
settled at Harvard in order to enjoy the spiritual neighborhood
of the Shakers.

An unplanned continuity has linked together the religious
and secular enterprises because many intellectuals believe that
they can make their own contribution to the betterment of man's
plight or the salvation of the soul. The scholar is made of the
same human stuff as the confessor and the social reformer; the
psychological traits that distinguish among the three differ so

slightly that any one of them may change his career into that of the other, and chance events may determine which of the three labels is tagged on a person. In any case, a number of scholars did announce missionary messages and left behind their testimony of books and deeds.

Back in the age of enthusiasm, Amos Comenius, a man with the fame of learning, and Nicholas Drabik, a man with the fame of martyrdom, heard heavenly voices and saw celestial visions portending that Protestantism will be exalted through Prince Rakoczi of Transylvania; they urged the Prince to take up arms in the defense of the faith, which he did and lost his battle, princedom, and life. In a different epoch Auguste Comte began his career by expounding the system of positivistic philosophy, then gave it up to found a religion of his own making with himself as the chief priest and his lady friend as the chief priestess; after years of labor he could find no more than twelve believers, and even this number might be exaggerated since twelve is a holy number for disciples in any Christian country. Sir Francis Galton, a man of many parts, founded mathematical statistics as well as eugenics which in his design turned out to be not a clear-cut science but a blueprint for the modern Utopia.

Did all these men pursue unattainable goals? Or is the scholar's success reduced by the extent of his missionary work? But Brodzinski is a successful and affluent confessor of faith similar in this respect to Sir Francis or, let us say, Dr. Edward Teller. Without any intent of flippancy, the notion of affluence leads my thoughts across the Atlantic and fixes them upon the American scene. Teller, this remarkable figure of Hungarian-American scholarship, is a part of the history of our times. The geographical adjective might be diminutive for him; on account of his influence he belongs to the whole world. His fame (as Julius Rezler so astutely analyzes it) rests not only on his accomplishments in physics but also on his stand; he has a particular place in the heart of a great many Americans because he represents a cause articulately, persistently, unswervingly.

What I know about Dr. Teller comes mostly from his meditative autobiography, and it is to his credit that in an age of mass communication, atomic censorship, and ghost-writing he can present us an autobiography so candidly revealing. "The main purpose of this book is," he states in the introduction, "to make my contribution to the cause of peace. . . . There are a few points which are obvious, but which are rejected by the majority of our people." The two short sentences ring with a resonance that the incidental linkage of words cannot achieve. The reader has to bring his attention to a rest and mull over the disarming simplicity of the text. The majority resists the truth about peace; fortunately enough, the author dedicates himself to the good cause of standing up for the obvious but rejected truth. Is this not the quintessence of every messianistic program which is designed for all people?

The following paragraphs spell out the obvious but rejected points: "In a dangerous world we cannot have peace unless we are strong. We cannot be strong unless we are fully prepared to exploit the biggest modern power, nuclear explosives. Nuclear weapons can be used with moderation on all scales of serious conflict. Nuclear weapons do not mean the end of the world. . . . The atomic age has brought fears, and it has brought a challenge. Unless we respond to the challenge, unless we create a world of tomorrow better than anything we can imagine or describe, too many of our fears will be justified."

Teller takes up the good cause of peace by pleading for nuclear armament. By all means his plea is not like the never-ceasing argument of military men for obtaining greater striking power, it is not like the practical proposition of diplomats for obtaining effective means in international power politics. Teller pleads in terms of a cosmic vision which regards nuclear weaponry as a necessary part of the better world of tomorrow. He speaks as a missionary who explores the future while the populace fix their eyes upon the present.

No man would set out for the mission without an inner encouragement. The missionary receives a calling, a sort of secret message, not given to others but conveyed to him in a special manner. "I still had not decided that I should devote myself to work on weapons," Teller relates his searching mood at a turning point of his career when the Congress of Pan-American Scientists came up with President Roosevelt scheduled as its festive speaker. Teller had no desire to hear "any political speech," but, as chance had it, on the same day Hitler invaded the Netherlands and to this news Teller responded in the same way as Americans in all walks of life did—he wanted to hear what the President had to say. "President Roosevelt's remarks carried a special significance for me," Teller continues with his recollections. "I concluded that President Roosevelt was telling us that the duty of scientists was to see that the most effective weapons would be available for use if necessary, that we would stand morally guilty before the free world if we refused to lend our talents to the cause of the free world. President Roosevelt's talk answered my last doubts. I left the meeting feeling that I was committed to do whatever I could."

Roosevelt, the eloquent president, knew how to appeal to Americans in all walks of life; yet, there is something wondrous, short of incredible, in the claim that his words—directed to scientists and ordinary citizens alike—redefined the aims of scholarship for a man from sophisticated Academe. But every conversion experience is wondrous, and this was Teller's conversion experience, basically similar to Paul's vision on the road to Damascus, to Augustine's hearing the heavenly voice, "Tolle, lege," and to the experiences of Mother Ann Lee, Father Rapp, Peter Veregin, and others of lesser names. In all these instances an unusual person received a somewhat vague, personal and unique stimulus that would not have changed and converted other people, but in the given person and under the given circumstances it worked miracles and created changes of lasting effect; it sent the chosen man to dedicate the whole of his life to a mission and make a few obvious points acceptable to the majority. Roosevelt's words reached Teller at the right moment, resolved his last doubts, and prompted him for a "moral decision."

The conversion experience ends with a decision; the converted man changes from an outsider into an insider and joins a tightly knit group; from now on he partakes in the brotherhood of the other confessors and shares their dedication to the common cause. It would be indiscreet to speculate about how strongly Teller was affected by the general human desire to be an insider, but it is obvious that through his decision he became an American beyond that shadow of a doubt that sometimes falls upon the person of foreign birth; he became very American and the protagonist of millions in this country.

If his conversion experience needed any reinforcement, the visions opened up by atom physics furnished it. The work on splitting the atom was like retracing the course of creation and inspired a reverential fear similar to religion. William L. Lawrence, a hard-boiled newspaperman, saw the explosion of the first atomic bomb at Alamogordo on the dawn of July 16, 1945, and exclaimed: "It was like being witness to the Second Coming of Christ!" The members of the scientific team, he noted, felt a similar awe because they "had shared in a profound religious experience, having been witness to an event akin to supernatural."

The test explosion signaled a historical achievement for science and a personal achievement for those who had been engaged in atomic development; it augured the end of the war and the return of peace. Yet, it left many of the scientists with a tragical feeling, a gnawing doubt whether their achievement was the work of good or evil. On its eve, J. Robert Oppenheimer quoted the sacred book of the Hindus, "I am become Death, the Shatterer of Worlds!" And George B. Kistiakowsky commented: "This was the nearest to doomsday one can possibly imagine. I am sure that at the end of the world—in the last millisecond of the earth's existence—the last man will see something very similar to what we have seen." Since that historical dawn in the desert land of New Mexico, the atomic eschatology haunted the minds of the best of the scholars, and the more they knew about nuclear physics, the more preoccupied they became with the possibility of a man-made Judgment Day.

Hiroshima, Nagasaki, and the surrender of Japan followed Alamogordo within a month. The labor of the atomic scientists accomplished everything that human force can accomplish and perhaps more, something of formidably superhuman proportions. The stage was set for messianism; but who would take the role offered by history itself? The scientific community of the Los Alamos Laboratory was breaking up. Most of its members looked at the atom as a wartime device and emergency construct that should be forgotten together with the other horrors of war. They were now ready to return to the peaceful pursuits of conventional academic life. Teller, however, could not agree with the viewpoints of his fellow scholars. As he reasoned, the atom was here to stay with us as a steady companion of mankind. Since peace is but a brief transition between two wars, the atom must not be forgotten and put aside but developed in its further potentials so that our capacity of possible destructiveness should remain perfectly manageable and should any time surpass the same capacity of other nations. Accordingly, Teller decided upon the goal of his future work: "the development of a hydrogen bomb or refinement of atomic explosions."

Perseverance and even stubbornness are necessary parts of missionary work, and as Teller looked around in the post-war world, he could discern many signs that apparently justified his unswerving stand. He could see a clearly anti-American power structure emerging on the international scene and could see doubts rising in the American mind about the external and internal security of the country. He could see the hitherto secret atom develop into a matter of national and international concern and, above all, could see messianistic scientists bestirring themselves on the opposite side of the atomic contest. The scholarly spies Allan Nunn May (the British physicist working in Canada), Klaus Fuchs (the uncommunicative genius who seemed to be equally at home in many countries of two continents), and Hsueshen Tsien (the mysterious rocket expert whom American immigration authorities detained lest he would reveal our secrets to China) discarded the freedom of Academe for the orders of the Party; took ignominy, danger, jail, and possible death in stride because they had cast their belief in the Communist credo.

What the scholarly spies did was correct by the standards of the Communist creed which impose upon scholars the ultimate duty of promoting the goals of the party state. But their deeds aroused consternation and disgust in non-monolithic America which, as a rule, is rather indulgent toward the men of learning. America, the country of many creeds, was now as unanimous as she ever could be, and her two main parts came to an amazingly close agreement. The Emersonian America, this defender of the idealistic creed of the nineteenth century that always viewed scholarship as a dedication to the objective search of truth, was now embarrassed to see that a few men of learning debased professional duties, sacrificed academic independence, and traded knowledge for messianistic zeal. The plain, common-sense America, this staunch admirer of the practical know-how that always preferred knowledge in its simple homey forms, reacted now with open dismay because she saw Nunn, Fuchs and Tsien as the modern Brutuses with the lean and hungry looks, betraying their friend and protector. Was it not significant (so common-sense America clamored) that the scholarly spies had been born abroad and had come as sojourners to this country? Was it for nothing that their conversion experience had been prompted by the words of Stalin and could not be altered by any American words? Was it not imperative that their un-American messianism should be countered with a messianism of the American kind?

We should not ruminate on how Teller reacted to the case of the spies, two of whom counted among his personal acquaintances. A determined mind does not need any public prompting. The moral decision he made upon hearing Roosevelt's words did not leave room for hesitation, and the program of the perfectly manageable destructiveness demanded categorical answers anyhow. Teller sided with common-sense America when most of his colleagues, the Oppenheimers, Bethes, Szilards, chose to stay with Emersonian idealism. He proceeded on his mission, doing his work with amazing effectiveness amidst the intricacies of political power structure and scientific production. He established contact with the men of power, Senator McMahon, Lewis Strauss, General Doolittle, and accomplished much in his office. When in June, 1951, the Atomic Energy Commission called a round-table conference of top scientists at the Princeton Institute for Advanced Study, Teller walked to the blackboard and presented the detailed calculations for building the hydrogen bomb.

The plan could not be delayed; it had to be completed in Teller's terms. "A strong second laboratory was needed," he argued, "to provide healthy competition in the thermonuclear field." Hence, the Livermore Laboratory was established and it became Teller's scientific home and a source of competition in work and policy. Soon there were "two schools of thought" concerning tactical weapons. One policy was summed up by Hans A. Bethe, one of the leaders at Los Alamos: "The Los Alamos Laboratory is generally of the opinion that we have reached very nearly the end of the road, that not much more can be obtained in the way of weapons improvement. They will admit that you can always make some further improvement, but here arises the question, Is it worthwhile?" The other school of thought represented by Livermore, was summed up by Teller: "Appeasement on our side and confident expansion on the side of the Communists have been the dominant themes of the post-war years. This situation must be changed. . . . Properly prepared, we can survive a nuclear attack. Having survived, we must be able to strike the second blow."

I do not propose to follow the subsequent phases of the national controversy on armament policy; my interest is limited to a personal aspect of the problem. Our historians and journalists are used to analyzing the personalities of the policy makers, yet, we pay little attention to the personalities of the ideology makers. But can we subsume the scientist under this presumptuous name? Am I not carried away by the suggestive power of C. P. Snow when I read messianistic aims into the actions of Dr. Teller? After all, physics carries an authority, a special aura that emanates far beyond the confines of campuses and laboratories. Physics is the model of sciences, a closed logical system cast into the lucid sequence of mathematical formulae, and the physicist is the model of scientists, a man of strict reasoning, unprejudiced and unemotional, who keeps his human frailties under control.

Others should judge whether this model can truly be applied to Newton, Boyle, and the renowned members of the Royal Society, many of whom maintained a close friendship with Comenius and Drabik. I think it is foolish to ignore the human element in any field of scholarship; the same laws of human behavior govern the public theories and the private lives of scientists. See how the last war has changed the status of physics and, in general, of science. War has turned into an affair of logistic, technology, and science, and whoever could enlist the most of martial scholarship, could confidently look forward to victory. Warfare has become scientific; the military men turned their interest from the brawny to the brainy and invited organization men, scholars, and intellectuals to join in the war efforts.

The German intellectuals responded to the invitation with the same enthusiasm as once the students of Fichte had done; brainy engineers designed gas chambers, medicine men used human guinea pigs, and rocketry experts worked on punitive weapons for Hitler and later for the Arab countries. In the American setting, however, the scientist was still an Emersonian idealist whose mind was not geared to missionary messages and could not be swayed by conversion experiences. He was likely to respond to the military invitation in the manner of Oppenheimer and Bethe, offer his knowledge to the war effort as a matter of temporary duty, but reserve his permanent obligation to the scholarly conscience, this scrutinizing, sometimes hesitant but always anxious guide of the trained mind. He did his duty in war, but war was not his duty; he was led not by a few obvious points but by the many interlocking principles that move patriots, scholars, and men.

Against this background the figure of Teller stands out, a "lonely figure" as one reporter described him; but any loneliness can refer to his missionary stance and not to his actual relationship with fellow citizens. His views are shared by millions all over the country, by politicians in Washington and men on the street in Dallas and Indianapolis. His fame rests not only on his scientific achievements but also on his ability to express the unformulated fears and desires of millions. Altogether, he is more than a successful scientist; he is a spokesman and a symbol with a tremendous influence outside the proper realm of science, in that territory where public manipulation, mission, and messianism lie.

Physics, this model of sciences, entails a great mental rigor upon its workers, but other disciplines follow more lenient rules and permit their students to weave personal wishes and dreams into the fabric of the subject matter. As C. P. Snow or, for that matter, Julius Rezler hint, we should think of political science as the model of the imaginative disciplines which manages to mix facts and dreams in its specific way. Political science is indeed the very counterpart of the logical consistency and material concreteness of physics; it has few rules or, if you like, little methodology; it covers a wide range of topics and is open to almost any soul willing to deal with it. In many parts of the world, political science denotes the Machiavellian art of furnishing the men of power with those facts and ideas that the men of power wish to obtain. If a country by chance happens to have two sets of men of power, it is likely to have two political sciences facing each other like parties in dispute like the school of Fichte, Treitschke, and Nietzsche faced that of Marx, Lassalle, and Bebel in old Germany, the school of the Slavophiles faced that of the revolutionaries in old Russia.

The classical political science of Europe, digressive, disputative, and rhetorical as it was, usually revolved around two issues —the matter of social justice and the legitimation of the existing governmental system. These were burning issues indeed in Germany, Russia, and a score of minor countries which were not only semi-feudal and undemocratic but also proudly obstinate in their opposition to any equality and democracy in the Anglo-Saxon sense of the words. But how could those issues be discussed, let alone settled, on any other basis than that of self-interest? They evoked a perennial disagreement between the haves and the have-nots, the insiders and the outsiders, since each party considered his side only and disregarded the other. American observers of these political disputations have been all too often shocked by the Marxist propositions put forward in the name of the have-nots. They tend to forget that the conservative propositions, given in the name of the haves, were just as prejudiced, and the two leading conservatives of the 1930's, Othmar Spann, the Austrian professor, and Salazar, the schoolmasterly dictator of Portugal, were not more palatable to the American taste with their thesis of an aristocratic minority being the natural guardian of morality, entitled by divine right to dole out social justice to the populace.

On this side of the Atlantic the fireworks of European political science were observed but not imitated. The pragmatic American mind recoiled from the grand theories of the European speculators; left it to strangers, Tocqueville and Lord Bryce, to interpret our own political system on a philosophical scale; and turned its interest to the problems of the here and now. When compared to Europe, politics in America appeared as provincial, and (as one may still notice in some of the southern states) political science often did not exceed the feelings of local patriotism and the knowledge of the local lore. The grave European issues failed to kindle the professorial passions, and for good reasons. The problem of social justice had little appeal in

America where the avenues of social mobility were not blocked by the remnants of medieval feudalism and where any young man had a chance to realize the national dream of fair success in life. The justification of the existing governmental system did not need the mental gymnastics of professors because American government represented a practical compromise among the many interest groups of the country and offered a workable system of democracy.

The philosophy of isolationism, pragmatic and provincial as it was, served as a solid foundation of half of our political science. It suited the American temperament so much that a very un-American and very international event was needed to change the country's mind. Nothing less than World War II could do it, nothing less than the agony of the battlefields closely followed by a national shock—the sudden emergence of the problem of Communism and national security. A war-weary nation that hoped for a peaceful life in the home towns saw itself unexpectedly confronted with a problem that could not be handled in homey American terms because it raised grave questions and demanded global answers. The nation could not avoid recognizing its insufficiency: it lacked that kind of political scientists that would be able to deal with the grave questions. In the same painful moment of self-examination it also realized that the refugee camps, these cheap market places of manpower, teemed with experts who claimed to possess the needed know-how. But what was the guarantee that the knowledge of these refugee experts, if imported to America, would furnish the right answers? In a second painful moment the nation realized that the whole content of life was tightly tied in with the problem of Communism and national security, and, as the first extemporized solution of the problem, any person entering the country had to be examined by the guardsmen of American thinking and national safety.

This was the reasoning that became embodied in the McCarran-Walter Immigration Act. It turned out to be a controversial piece of legislation, often blamed for rejecting innovations and preserving the old national quota system in admitting immigrants; strangely enough, its critics have apparently overlooked that the bill did introduce a novel principle—the examination of people's ideologies. The bill required security clearance and sponsorship as conditions of admission for immigrants; in practical application it required the selection of immigrants by their anti-Communist ideologies. The would-be immigrant from a low-quota country (and almost all Communist-dominated countries had low admission quotas) had to convince the American authorities that he was animated by nothing but lifelong anti-Communist feelings, and the greater anti-Communism he could manifest before the authorities, the better chances he had (or believed to have) to be admitted to the land of promise.

One may ask whether it is wise to apply ideological commitment as the chief criterion in admitting or rejecting immigrants; one may bring up more questions about whether a bureaucratic machinery such as our immigration service can reach a satisfactory appraisal of the ideological fitness of aliens. The fact that a great number of former Communist party members were admitted, while an equally great number of applicants who had never been party members were rejected, raises some doubts about the appropriateness of the ideological processing of immigrants. Further doubts might be raised about the social justice involved. Former politicians, civil servants, and army officers managed to prove their anti-Communist stand easily, but former peasants and workers, whose life had not hinged on ideological commitment, found it extremely hard to prove themselves and obtain admission to the United States.

The arriving immigrants, whatever their persuasion in the old country had been, were likely to read into the admission procedure a meaning that the makers of the law hardly intended to give. The refugees interpreted the security clearance and sponsorship as conferring on them a special commission, withheld from the not-cleared and not-sponsored people in the country. They felt commissioned to assume the authority of teaching, advising and leading Americans in the problem of Communism and national security. They were eager to fulfill this assignment in civic action, teaching, or any other activity where their interest, background, or the chance led them. Thus, a great many of them ended up in political science and especially in its timely branch, Sovietology. Some of them, having been lawyers and civil servants in Europe, had a doctorate in political science; others, having been politicians and newspaper reporters, acquired a practical knowledge in politics; others again, by the sheer virtue of knowing their native country, qualified as area experts, a new kind of specialist whose usefulness increases as world politics becomes more diffused and countries, unheard-of a short time ago, demand a role in international affairs.

Political science, the lenient discipline with liberal entrance requirements, tried to accommodate the newcomers in the field. The established seats of scholarship absorbed but a few novices; the small colleges hired more, including some with titled names, and mixed the nobilitarian and academic titles of their staff into a new color in the collegiate rainbow. On the fringes of respectable Academe a new variety of organized scholarship opened up and proffered generous opportunities to the novices. The national interest in Soviet affairs prompted government agencies, business firms, immigrant groups, and entrepreneurial-minded individuals to found research institutes, academies, reviews dedicated to Sovietology; and out of the many occasional enterprises, the Radio Free Europe, for example, grew into an organization of imposing size and durability. To be sure, the fringe scholarship did not exactly follow the Emersonian ideals but was likely to be engaged in activities to which a sophisticated parlance might apply the names of propaganda, public relations, lobby, pressure group and, perhaps, intelligence; but such a diversification in itself proved the timeliness and popularity of organized Sovietology.

Within this total setting any intellectual persistent enough found himself a place. One of those *Who's Who's* which list the eminent members of an ethnic group contains the biographies of some 250 people (that is, 4 per cent of all the personages listed) who at one point of their career have worked as Communist experts. From the biographies a composite picture of amazing occupational mobility emerges in which political science was not a lifetime occupation but a temporary stage in changeable and altogether not entirely unsuccessful career. Here is the former army officer who upon his arrival in America published many articles on "Russia and its Satellites," "Sabotage and Espionage in Peace and War," and then settled down as an evidently prominent member of a metropolitan real estate board;

the clergyman and missionary in China who in America became an expert on the political philosophy of Mao Tse-tung and television engineering; the aristocrat, sport executive and band leader who in between managed to head the research section of an institute dealing with Eastern Europe; the former lawyer, cabinet minister, émigré politician, now a frequent lecturer at international conferences, author of a book of memoirs as well as articles in *Reader's Digest, Saturday Evening Post,* and *Stag*; the former lawyer and local politician working in America with a Mid-European Research Center and subsequently with the forestry service.

Perhaps it never happened before that the country—or any country of the world—had so many experts occupied with the same problem of political science, and theirs was an ideologically selected group of experts who had undergone the same conversion experience and were passionately involved in their subject matter. Their aim was not study but action. They addressed the lay public with the intention of mobilizing the little old lady in tennis shoes and the retired accountant in California. Their knowledge, to be sure, was more serviceable to community leaders and citizens with leisure time than to established scholars, and they used this knowledge for initiating actions, organizing civic protests, demonstrations, and letter-writing campaigns to editors and congressmen. They were not deterred by the fact that against the hard reality of world politics the civic protest can hardly be more than a community ritual; they were animated by a Tellerian mission of knowing a few obvious points about which the skeptical majority was unwilling to do something.

The scattered evidences of their work bear testimony to their missionary zeal. One foreign-born professor of political science, as he stated before a newspaper reporter, traveled 30,000 miles between California and Maine and delivered 150 lectures on the Communist menace to civic groups, church organizations, and PTA's. "Communism is the greatest threat to America," the professor said, and added, "most Americans close their eyes before this danger." The professor was not the only traveling expert. Another clipping from a campus newspaper is about a hooded refugee addressing the student body and wearing the hood to protect his family in the native country against the revenge of the Communist police; the address, however, divulged his former place of employment which would enable any police worth their wages to establish his identity. As another testimony I have a mimeographed leaflet issued at the time when the students of Princeton University invited Alger Hiss for a talk. It urged "every red-blooded American . . . and every loyal Princetonian to write in and protest the supiness (!) of the present Princeton administration and its utter contempt for decency and the finer sensibilities of fellow Americans." This protest against the soft-on-Communism Ivy League was thrust into my hands, not by a loyal Princetonian and not by an entirely red-blooded American, but by a foreign-born Sovietologist.

Our academic world is inclined to regard publication as proof of scholarship, and the foreign-born expert rated high by this standard. He was a voluble exponent of the message; his list of publications would be long enough to please any academic committee. One of them claimed to have turned out during 15 years of American residence some 500 articles in 14 languages. According to another report, Radio Free Europe published in the course of three years 150 books, booklets, and pamphlets in English, to which one might add further publications in other languages. I do not know how the general public received such a torrent of publications, but the scholarly journals usually refused to take notice of them. I doubt that one example would be representative of the whole mass, but one book was reviewed by a number of journals and can be assessed by someone not familiar with the subject matter.

The book, entitled *Hungary*, was edited by two professors of reputable affiliations and published under the direction of Radio Free Europe. One of its reviewers counted "almost a hundred" errors in the 22 pages of one chapter, while another critic described it as "an error-per-page book." Some errors are small-sized and might be attributed to the editors' evident ignorance of Hungarian; others are of considerable magnitude and must be ascribed to a fundamental confusion regarding the geography and history of the country. The general impression is hardly improved by the report that several exiled politicians instituted libel suits against the book, nor by the opinion of some readers who claim to have discovered recurrent undertones of racial and religious prejudice in the text.

Is it altogether just that one should apply academic standards to a book of message? The requirements of painstaking scholarship must be plainly inhibitive for anybody with a sense of mission. It has absolutely no bearing on his case whether the geographical and historical data are straight because the data could not alter the fact that Communism is morally wrong. It is superfluous for him to use more than two categories in judging exiled politicians and red-blooded Americans because someone is either for or against the message, and whoever is against it must be a Communist anyhow. The writer of scholarship and the writer of message use two different ways of reasoning, and while a scholar of the Teller type is not reduced in stature when he preaches the evangelism of manageable destructiveness, the missionary cannot be redoubled with scholarship by attributing him the arcane knowledge of a few obvious points.

The immigrant expert on Communist affairs sincerely believed, and told us ever so often, that his points were rejected by the majority; yet, I doubt that he has experienced much personal or ideological rejection. In fact, he has succeeded more than any other type of immigrants—the émigrés of the French revolution, the Germans of 1848, the Czechs of World War I—in commanding the attention of the public and exerting a deep influence upon the American mentality. Thus, a greater than usual cautiousness is necessary when evaluating his work; but this evaluation must somehow be attempted because no intellectual toil can be fully understood without placing it in its proper perspective. The refugee Sovietologist deserves much praise as a missionary and activist. With his emotional appeal he aroused a general interest in Soviet affairs at a time when isolationism was still popular and indifference toward foreign countries was still great in America. In his own ways he contributed to our knowledge of Communist affairs at a time when this contribution was most needed; he helped to raise a generation of American-educated Sovietologists who then could apply the standards of academic scholarship to this branch of political science.

As the foremost merit, he helped to shape a new American

ideology at a time when the old Emersonian traditions declined in popularity. As World War II ended, the old, inner-directed national ideology, which viewed America in itself, as a land of unlimited opportunities and a worthy substitute for the world at large, this noble and self-confident provincialism, suddenly proved to be insufficient and ill-suited and left the citizens unprepared to cope with the disturbing events of the world. A fresh, other-directed ideology was needed, a new formula of global terms that could sum up in one sweeping statement Ohio, Byelorussia, and Kashmir and present the correct answers to commonsense America. The immigrant political scientist happened to arrive amidst the country's general mood of re-examination, doubtfulness, and insecurity. With a sensitivity frequent among strangers, he sensed the opportunity of the moment; with the expressiveness of the professional politician, he prepared a felicitous answer; with the institutional support given to him, he carried the message across the country; and, in final analysis, he forcefully shaped the American philosophy on national survival in the cold war.

The general content of his ideology is simple and unsophisticated, as missionary messages are apt to be. It is an ideology based on the vision of arms which selects one out of the many possible answers to the Communist challenge and refuses to entertain any other answer. It disowns the view that Russia or China should be regarded as America's powerful rivals, and treated according to the eternal craft of power politics, that the policy toward any Communist country should be flexible, changing with the circumstances and utilizing the whole diplomatic gamut from conciliation to cold war. The new ideology sets a few elementary tasks before America: on the external front the liberation of the "captive nations" and the establishment of non-Communist governments in every country of the world; on the home front, an effective militancy against those Americans who would recommend, let alone employ, any other policy. In brief, our policy must be manifest hostility on the external front and never-resting suspicion at home.

This is a simple missionary message. It appeals to many former refugees whose vision of American arms includes a triumphant return to the native country that they had been forced to leave.

It appeals to many Americans—the followers of the plain common sense or the McCarthy-Goldwater minority of the country—who cannot tolerate uncertainties and ambiguities, applaud the elementary formulas and rally to fight for them. Naturally, the utter simplicity of the message requires that the whole arena of world politics be stripped of its numberless intricate problems and be reduced to the tidiness of a nursery. It is not enough to rewrite the geography of Hungary; the whole world map has to be redrawn, and all the facts of international politics have to be re-interpreted to fit the notion of one pasture for white sheep and another pasture for black sheep. My impression is that one brand of imported Sovietology, supported as it was by the fringe of our scholarly enterprise, was willing to do that; it tended to mislead the Americans about the Soviet affairs and the foreigners about the essence of America; altogether, it contributed to that basic misunderstanding which divides our world.

Many of the immigrant Sovietologists were unable to resist the temptation that human wishes, self-deception, and self-interest pose to the scholar. They failed to remove sufficiently enough the bias from their judgment; they saw the world as they wished to see it, underestimating Soviet power and belittling its achievements. They tended to impress upon American public opinion that nothing but terror upholds the Communist state, that the general dissatisfaction is ready to erupt in a popular revolution, that the Soviet system is bound to collapse any minute. Similarly, they tended to exaggerate any fault, inefficiency, or incompetence of Soviet production, organization, social welfare, and education. In the summer and fall of 1957 the American press hammered away on the backwardness of Russian science and education, on the primitive genetics of Comrade Lysenko and the Patomkin-like schools of engineering; small wonder that it created something like a national shock in America when the Sputnik was put into orbit.

It was perhaps just an unanticipated consequence of this militant ideology that the immigrant Sovietologist tended to misrepresent the image of America. Whether he addressed the American public or any of the peoples on five continents who came within range of our international propaganda, he insisted on the American duty of fighting Communism in every country

and on the home front as well. All too often he ended up by con-
juring the image of the American as the trigger-happy cowboy
with two Colts in the holster, ready to shoot anybody who dis-
agrees on matters of ideology. The great American heritage of
liberalism and tolerance, the spirit of compromise as the essential
feature of our politics were likely to be lost in his presentation,
and the foreign audience which did not share his commitment
but viewed world politics as less simple and less messianistic were
led by his words to visualize the figure of the ugly American.

One may rightly argue that this was so because America wanted
to be misled and was greatly pleased by the whole process involved; this indeed is one possible explanation of that public
success that the immigrant political scientist made. A great many
Americans wished to hear the missionary message, wished to ignore the Soviet as a power on the international scene, and wished
to enjoy that simple certainty and psychological relief that the
ideology gave in our troubled era. The immigrant scholar expressed what many native-born wanted to hear; by expressing
the slumbering wishes, he clarified and reinforced them and,
altogether, increased the anti-Communist feelings of the masses.
He did not create the strong popular desire for a national American mission, but he did refine, verbalize, and popularize the
militant ideology of fighting at home and abroad till the final
defeat of Communism.

This is the point where I have to return to my opening question about the feasibility of messianism in our century, an epoch
that we have adorned with a great many adjectives. Ours is a
scientific century, but our progress in sciences has made the
picture of the world even more confusing to the man on the
street. This is an affluent century, but the spoiled suburbanite
desires miracles just as much as the old Kentucky farmer did at
the revival meeting. This is a psychotherapeutically-oriented
century, but the restlessness of the soul is just as common now
as it was any time before Freud, and perhaps even more common because this is the century of mass societies when everybody
has a burning desire to differ, even though in a matter as small
as the dot of the *i*, from the rest of the mass.

The social conditions of our century do not remove the psychological necessity of messianism. The self-confidence of hav-

ing a mission, the certainty of knowing a few obvious points that others do not know, the work of convincing the majority—all these elements correspond to the basic human needs of every epoch and country. Perhaps the content of the few obvious points have changed with time; in the past they were mainly religious, at present they are mainly secular, nationalistic, and socialistic. In the past the theologian and the interpreter of the Bible were supposed to know them; at present, the physicist and the political scientist. There has been no change in the necessity of messianism; but a new type of missionary has emerged, the man who received his call to mission through some kind of secular scholarship. By this change the scholar has been encouraged to do a more active missionary work than the colleagues of Comenius and Comte did.

A messianistic program is feasible in our century provided it can find expedient scholars who verbalize its content and carry it to the masses; it is feasible provided it does not follow the spontaneous and innocent evangelism of the past, but enlists the support of the learning, logistics, and organizational know-how of the present era and, with their help, builds up a social movement. America, the historical country of evangelistic missionaries, recognized this truth at a turning point of her history. As the last war drew to its close and the appropriate time for reformulating her national mission emerged, the needed experts were missing and native-born scholarship withdrew from the required work on scientific messianism. But the country utilized its managerial sophistication and immediately came up with a practical solution: if the local supply could not meet the demand for manpower, the latter had to be moved in from other areas.

So the immigrant came. His ideological scholarship obtained in continental Europe and our ideological clearance given to him upon arrival equipped him to meet the current demand and take up work in organized Sovietology. Whatever he afterward did, he made his contribution to America's history over the last two decades. One must not trifle with his role because this role is independent of the scholarly standards he used, the ideology he manufactured, and the policy he recommended. This role depends on the loud echo that his words found in America, on the popularity he achieved, on the vote of confidence he received from the little old lady in tennis shoes and the retired accountant in California. This role is more than a matter of current popularity, it is an eternal part of human nature. As long as arms and visions will have a part in politics and humanity will use force and war in settling disputes, mankind will need messianistic scholars to give respectability to human dreams, wishes, and furies.

JOHN M. MUNRO

Out of the Tower and into the Arena

An Account of Some of the Problems
Facing English Teachers at American Universities

IN RECENT YEARS there has been much talk in the English Parliament and press concerning the so-called "brain drain," the departure from Britain of large numbers of highly qualified young men who, after receiving their education at home, decide to take up positions overseas. Although statistics are not available, the number must be fairly large, especially for those who go to the United States with the idea of making university teaching their career, because competition for university positions in England is fierce and the remuneration for the successful ones not particularly high. Nevertheless, it is likely that the number of English university teachers in the humanities at American universities does not exceed that of expatriate scientists, partly because the demand for scientists is greater, but for other reasons, too, which have an important bearing on some of the problems which English university teachers have to face in trying to adjust to the American scene.

In the first place, while in England the prestige of American science is high, it is still generally believed that the United States is something of a cultural wasteland. Secondly, the difference between the salary of a young English scientist and that of his American counterpart is much greater than that of a young English university lecturer and an instructor in the United States. Thirdly, a scientist who goes to the United States expects to gain valuable experience which will stand him in good stead if ever he wishes to return home, while a person who goes to the United States to take up a position in a humanities department at a university knows that he will have to distinguish himself extraordinarily if he is to attract attention in England. Finally, a scientist can be persuaded to go to the United States by the promise of greater opportunities and superior facilities for research, while it is felt, erroneously, that research in the humanities is next to impossible if one does not have relatively easy access to the British Museum or the Bibliothèque Nationale.

In short, all this means that the young English scientist can depart for the United States confident that whether he likes the country or not, the experience will be both personally and professionally rewarding, while the Englishman who comes to teach the arts at an American university tends to feel that he is burning his bridges behind him—that once he takes up his position the chances of his teaching in an English university are faint. Therefore, the majority of Englishmen who do come to teach at universities in the United States do so not from choice but necessity. Admittedly, there are many Englishmen who come out of curiosity, or to pursue a particular branch of research for which facilities are available, but they tend to be visitors only, away from home for a year, their posts in England assured. It is also true that some married men with growing families come to the United States because their salaries at home are insufficient to meet their increasing economic needs. On the whole, however, English university teachers in the arts who come to the United States are here simply because they were unable to find satisfactory positions at home. Thus, they tend to be not of the highest quality, or if they are, are probably products of local grammar schools and provincial universities, who have found their lack of public school and Oxbridge training an impediment to their gaining the kind of position they would wish. In either case they are liable to feel rejected by the English system, and this may have some bearing on the way they react to their new environment.

Perhaps one should not stress this aspect of the English teacher's position unduly, but it may help to explain why many young Englishmen teaching in American universities find it difficult to adjust to their new university environment. As E. M. Forster noted in his *Passage to India*, the English colonial who at home would have been little more than a middle-class nonentity becomes, when transplanted in an alien culture, more English than the most tradition-bound, landed aristocrat. Similarly, I would suggest, the expatriate English university teacher in the United States tends to become an even more militant upholder of the English higher educational system than the most conservative Oxbridge don. Consequently, when confronted with the demands peculiar to the American university system, many Englishmen either find it difficult to fulfill them satisfactorily or obstinately refuse to try. For example, students at English universities are left considerably more on their own than those in America. It may be argued that this is a wasteful process because so many students lack the maturity of temperament to pursue their studies without close supervision; on the other hand, the practice may be defended on the grounds that it encourages a lively and responsible independence of thought and behavior. However, the point here is not to consider the relative merits of the English and American systems, but simply to note an essential difference. Thus, the Englishman teaching in America, his visions of English students' maturity and industriousness becoming rosier the longer he is away from home, frequently finds rather irksome the necessity of looking after his charges with an eye only a little less than paternal. He is liable to resent taking daily attendance; giving frequent "quizzes" to ascertain whether students have done their reading assignments; debating whether so-and-so may legitimately be excused from class to play football, sing with the Glee Club, or take part in other university activities; filling out progress reports for fraternities, athletic directors, deans, major departments, and sometimes for psychiatrists; preparing, when necessary, elaborate dossiers for such bodies as the Students' Honor Council when a student is suspected of cheating; and perhaps most of all, listening to students' problems, both personal and academic. All these things the Englishman tends to find irksome, and will probably resent that such duties are expected of him. Relatively unused to looking upon their students as individuals, many Englishmen will find such day-to-day demands unusually difficult to comply with, while others will look upon them as unnecessary, maintaining resolutely that the way students conduct their affairs is none of their business, and that their responsibility is to teach rather than to baby-sit.

Another difficulty which may cause resentment is the necessity of tailoring one's courses to meet the rather special requirements of American students. In an English university, students in a particular class will have had, more or less, the same kind of schooling; their ethnic, cultural and social backgrounds will tend to be similar; most of them will be working toward the same degree, to be granted the same year; and they will all have approximately the same motivation to study. Perhaps most significant of all, the majority of students in a particular class, and in many cases all of them, will be specializing in the subject being discussed, and will all know roughly the same about it. Accustomed to the homogeneity of the average class at an English university, the English teacher may feel completely overwhelmed when faced with the ethnic, social, and cultural assortment typical of most American classes, where students of varying abilities and enthusiasm are held together in uneasy synthesis for a semester. Obviously, if he has any hopes of reaching the majority in his classes, the English teacher will have to review and probably revise his lectures to conform to the general standard. This does not mean that he must necessarily lower his standards, though this to some degree is inevitable; it does mean, however, that he must endeavor to communicate whatever he has to say as clearly as possible, in terms that the students will readily understand. This is not simply a question of language, though a lecturer in America will probably feel the necessity to use a less erudite vocabulary than his English counterpart, but it also affects the method of presentation itself. In England, for example, a lecturer teaching English literature will generally assume that his students have understood what they have read, and he will also assume that they are aware that what the writer has said is worth saying. Thus, his lectures will tend to concentrate on various aspects of literary technique—how a writer has achieved a particular kind of effect—and how a writer's work fits into the context of the history of English literature. In short, he will tend to regard a particular writer or literary work in a purely literary context. In America, however, one is frequently faced with the problem of students not being able to understand what they are reading, and when they do, being unconvinced that their lives are made any the richer for it. Therefore, if one has any ambition to be more than simply a medium for the transmission of information, one must think of literature in the broadest possible terms, and, without appealing to literary precedents or standards, endeavor to show why such-and-such a piece of writing is great, and why a proper appreciation of it can be as rewarding for engineers as for English majors. Thus, a lecturer in England teaching, say, Shakespeare's dramas, would probably spend more time describing Elizabethan stage conventions, problems of Elizabethan language and rhetoric, Shakespeare's sources for his plays, the contemporary social and cultural background, and so on, than he would going through the plays in class, pointing to various felicities of expression, commenting on the appropriateness and effectiveness of particular speeches, and drawing attention to the significance of various passages not simply with reference to the play as a whole, but to human nature, contemporary society, and even to life itself. Certainly, many English lecturers in America tend to resent what they might be disposed to call "diluting" their lectures for the benefit of people whose interest in literature is either marginal or non-existent, and many are unable, or possibly refuse, to meet the level of their classes.

This inability or refusal to find a common level of sympathy or understanding with his classes is probably only one aspect of a larger issue which the Englishman has some difficulty in accepting: that higher education in America is dedicated to teaching the greatest number of students who may reasonably be expected to benefit from further study, rather than giving special consideration to a few. The lecturer in England is used to addressing small, elite groups of specialists; he expects them to understand his vocabulary, his literary allusions, his jokes, as well as the substance of his lectures. Inevitably, a club spirit prevails. Because everyone understands (or at least, pretends to understand) what is going on, and because the underlying assumptions regarding the usefulness of studying literature are taken for granted, there is no necessity to appeal to other than literary criteria to justify one's judgments or points of view. Classes tend to be less like sittings in a council chamber where there is a free interchange of personal points of view presided over by a good-natured chairman, which approximates to the

American ideal, than congregations of the elect coming together to take part in a quasi-religious ceremony under the aegis of an exalted high priest.

It is not surprising then, that a lecturer used to the decorum and dignified ceremony of an English university lecture frequently finds the informal atmosphere of a typical American class rather hard to endure. In English university classes the lecturer has few disciplinary problems. Late-comers are few, for those who cannot arrive on time generally prefer to forego the lecture entirely than enter the room after it has begun. Students are generally quieter, better mannered, and no matter how boring the lecture may be, only a few brave souls would dare to register their feelings with a sigh or a yawn. Certainly the behavior of American students in class is rather poor by any standards, and one can sympathize with the horror which many English visitors express concerning class conduct. Nevertheless, even supposing American students behaved with the same politeness as their English counterparts, the English lecturer would still have to cope with certain distractions which arise naturally from the traditional way classes are conducted in the United States. Before he enters a class the lecturer in England will have carefully prepared his material, budgeted his time, and in the classroom may deliver his lecture as one would read a paper, brooking no interruptions and, indeed, expecting none. In America, however, the lecturer must be prepared to answer questions, clarify and perhaps re-clarify his statements, suffer himself to be drawn into impromptu discussions allowing everyone his say. Although with practice one can control informal class exchanges without too much difficulty and without hurting too many feelings, it is a constant problem making sure one covers sufficient material. Consequently, the informality of American university classes may frequently distress English lecturers, who are likely to find class discussions both time-wasting and distracting, and, though few would admit it, an additional strain on their intellectual capacities.

The necessity to supervise students closely, the difficulties which result from the variable nature of American classes, and the informal class behavior, are probably the greatest bugbears of English university teachers in America. The degree to which these difficulties may be overcome will depend not only on the teacher's ability to conform to his new environment, but also on his willingness to recognize that the ideals and functions of British and American universities differ. If he is prepared to accept the fact that American higher education caters not simply to the elite few, but endeavors to provide instruction for as many who may reasonably be expected to benefit from it—in short, if he is prepared to acknowledge that what is different may not necessarily be inferior—then the English teacher in America will have overcome the greatest obstacle in the way of his adjustment. The fact that many Englishmen seem unable to accept this simple fact is perhaps partly due to the insecurity they seem to feel as a result of their being rejected by the English system.

There are, however, other problems which are liable to cause the English teacher in America some concern, but these arise not so much from the differences between the British and American university systems, as the attitudes of students and colleagues to English academics as a class. These difficulties may be summarily dealt with, as they tend to arise from their misconceptions of the English as a race.

The notion that professors are absent-minded and out of touch with life is universal, but rightly or not it is generally assumed that the English academic is, almost by definition, eccentric. There is some justification for such a view. One recalls professors who managed consistently to wear socks that did not match, or ill-fitting suits; one remembers professors with quaint, idiosyncratic speech mannerisms and odd quirks of behavior. Indeed, European society in general has come to expect, even demand, that its university professors display a few pardonable eccentricities, and academics have been ready to oblige. Even as a race the English are supposed to be rather odd, a view which British film comedies have been ready to exploit, and many young Americans especially are apt to feel that eccentricity is as characteristically British as thatched cottages, warm beer, and Stilton cheese. For English teachers in America this means that one's students, in their willingness to see the lighter side of life, are ready to regard one's most sober pronouncements as high comedy, coming to class to be entertained rather than instructed.

This certainly has its advantages, and it may be cautiously exploited as a useful teaching device, but there are always one or two students who are unable to determine where comedy leaves off and instruction begins.

However, one should not exaggerate the problems arising from American students' misconceptions of the English academic. After the first few meetings the notion that English university teachers are necessarily different from the American kind should have disappeared, and most students are intelligent enough to dissociate myth from reality. More complex, perhaps, than the relationship with one's students is the relationship with one's colleagues. To some extent they too subscribe to a mythical conception of the educated Englishman, not, however, the comic caricature which obtains among students, but to the legend that all English university teachers are witty, urbane dilettantes, superficially brilliant but lacking in intellectual depth. Thus one is expected to be amusing, fluent, gracious, and is indeed valued for these qualities if one possesses them, but at the same time one tends to be regarded as being incapable of real scholarly activity. Therefore, though many department chairmen would hesitate to formulate it thus, the acquisition of one or two Englishmen on the faculty is regarded as adding "tone" rather than substance, and one is never really sure whether one has been hired for one's nationality or for one's academic qualifications.

Finally, no discourse professing to deal with some of the problems which confront an English university teacher in America would be complete without some mention of "academic freedom." Without doubt an Englishman teaching at an English university is used to considerably more academic freedom than his American counterpart. One cannot conceive of a lecturer of English literature with avowed communist sympathies being allowed to teach at an American university at all, much less to present the history of the nineteenth-century English novel in terms of the class struggle. In England, however, there is such a man, and his academic career seems not to have been jeopardized on account of his political beliefs, nor, so far as I know, has his teaching been publicly condemned for its socialist bias. Nevertheless, to say that lack of academic freedom is a serious problem for Englishmen teaching in America would not be true, because the English academic tends to be less assertive, less involved with contemporary events, and not used to making controversial statements about political events or systems in class. Admittedly, many Englishmen in the United States will deplore the powers exercised by the university administration, the alumni, the state government, and other institutions to control and stifle a teacher's right to express what he believes, but one should not interpret their complaints as cries from the heart. For English teachers in America, questions about academic freedom tend to be little more than theoretical, and few, I think, could honestly maintain that it constituted a major problem for them.

This account of some of the problems that confront an English teacher at an American university is, of course, highly subjective, being based on my own experience and the experience of other Englishmen in a similar situation. But even as I write I cannot help thinking that perhaps, like Ezra Pound's M. Verog, I am "out of step with the decade." During the past four years new universities have been opened at a number of places, and of the more important ones—those at Brighton, Colchester, York, Coventry, Lancaster and Norwich—only York has chosen to follow closely the traditional British pattern. The others, in varying degrees, have all been influenced by American universities, most notably in their attempts to broaden the undergraduate curriculum and to limit specialization, but also in such relatively minor matters as, for example, the appointment of a writer in residence at Norwich. In short, if the pattern of the new universities is indicative of a national trend, the notion that humanities departments in British institutes of higher learning are cloistered havens for genteel dilettantes is bound to require revision. Furthermore, if the character of British universities is changing, and I rather think it is, it is likely that future generations of English university teachers will find teaching in the United States a less disorienting experience than it now seems for many. Even so, as long as Britain is able to grant the benefits of a higher education only to an elite few, and as long as a specialized education rather than a general one is the underlying principle on which a higher education in Britain is based, English teachers in America are bound to find some difficulty in adjusting to the requirements imposed upon them by the American system.

It may be felt that in drawing attention to some of the problems which confront the English university teacher in America I have presented too negative a picture. There are difficulties, to be sure, but there are rewards too. In England the study of literature tends to be a cloistered activity, with lecturers and students sharing in the common experience of enjoying good books. Because few would think of asking it, one is never required to answer the question, "is what I am doing worthwhile?" As a result, the study of literature tends to become increasingly detached from life and to take on the character of an esoteric pursuit. More and more one feels that it is little more than a gentlemanly pastime, designed to add polish and refinement to those about to enter the world to make a living, or to provide others with the necessary background to enable them to carry on the teaching of literature elsewhere. In America, however, where the university tends to be less of an ivory tower, one is constantly required to review and sometimes to reassess the fundamental principles on which one's whole career is based. Certainly teaching English literature at an English university is more "pleasant" than teaching it in America. Only the most partisan American scholar would deny that. Whether teaching English literature in England is as rewarding as teaching it in the United States is another matter. It is frustrating, to say the least, to feel an obligation to try and instill some appreciation for literature into people who, one feels, might be more profitably employed breaking stones than breaking their heads. Sometimes, however, in teaching students whom one has rather hastily dismissed as incorrigible morons, one will find that somehow one has penetrated to a core of unawakened sensibility and provoked a genuine response in regard to a particular writer or work of art. When this happens one's belief in the power of great literature to refine or illuminate what, for want of a better word, one might call the "soul," is reaffirmed; faith in the value of teaching and studying literature is renewed. In our technological society where only practical considerations seem to have much place, one soon begins to doubt whether the study of literature is really worthwhile. It needs a rather dramatic demonstration to make one believe that literature may still speak to others than those who have made it their career to listen to it, and in the American university one is more apt to experience it than in England. Complacent about his social usefulness an honest university teacher of literature in America can never be. And this is all to the good. With the proper approach, teaching literature to undergraduates in America can be a vastly stimulating experience, frustrating perhaps, but never dull.

SIEGFRIED WENZEL

Confrontation in the English Department

TO WRITE about the immigrant scholar who works in the field of English literature is to write about very small numbers indeed. In contrast to specialists in modern languages or in comparative literature, very few foreign-born professors of English have—during the past three decades or so—found their way into American universities. The reason for this is obvious: one does not usually go to a foreign country to teach the correct use of its language or the wealth of its literary inheritance. Yet there has been, in the past, a thin line of men born and sometimes fully educated in Europe who came to America to leave their stamp on the study of English. Frederick Klaeber, for example, whose edition of *Beowulf* has been at one time or another in the hands of every graduate student in English, was born in Prussia and studied at German universities. After receiving the Ph.D. from Berlin he accepted an offer to teach in the English Department at the University of Minnesota, where he worked in voluntary seclusion until his retirement. Another foreign-born scholar who has devoted his life to English linguistics is Hans Kurath, well known for his work on the *Linguistic Atlas of North America* and the new *Middle English Dictionary*. He was born in Austria but came to America as a child and received his university training here.

Such cases, however, are isolated and yield far too little material for generalizing statements. In addition, immigrant scholars who work in this particular field have come to America from such variegated backgrounds, at such differing stages of their intellectual development, and for so many diverse reasons, that it becomes almost worthless to speak of them as a group. It seems to me much more fruitful to reflect, simply and humbly,

161

on personal experiences, with the awareness that the following remarks may not at all apply to fellow immigrants.

To do so, however, appears to this writer as a rather embarrassing task. He is not experiencing his present life as a constant confrontation between himself and America. He is not acutely conscious of living in a foreign country whose peculiarities and mores he has to observe, judge, assimilate, or reject at every second of his waking hours. This may not make him a very good representative of the Immigrant Intellectual in America. On the other hand, it may be worthwhile meditating upon the causes of this state of affairs—subjective as well as objective—in order to elucidate what it has meant, in this particular case, to work as an immigrant scholar in the field of English literature.

The writer was born in Germany, where he passed through the normal pre-war primary and secondary school curriculum and had, after the war, a brief glimpse of the intellectual work at a university in Western Germany. He then followed his parents to South America, a step taken not for political but strictly economic reasons. There he undertook the normal four years' work of university study in English and German languages and literatures, preparing himself for a teaching position in a high school and, eventually, at the university. Good fortune brought him a scholarship for further study at a small state university in the American Middle West, and from there he progressed to a Ph.D. in English at one of America's mammoth state universities. Scholarly pursuits had always been his secret longing, and with the encouragement and help of kind teachers and friends he finally decided to stay. To him, an American university furnishes the best environment he needs to fulfill what he deems his life work: research and teaching. His background is, thus, more complex than that of the average immigrant. Successive adaptation to not one but two foreign cultures and the fact that he is not strictly a refugee or an exile are perhaps the primary reasons why he is not experiencing a split between himself as immigrant and America.

Other reasons can be sought in the reality which has confronted him ever since he came to America, a reality which has made adaptation a fairly easy and quick process. There is, first of all, the very great generosity with which Americans have received and welcomed the foreign intellectual, a generosity which by now is almost proverbial. It shows itself in many forms. On the level of the half-educated, it has brought crowds of eager women in search of culture to the feet of well-paid traveling lecturers and *littérateurs*, whose pronouncements they swallow with charming, if naive, enthusiasm. But this phenomenon is not restricted to America, and it is hardly relevant here, were it not that one often meets the same enthusiasm on a higher level within the university world. There is a widespread willingness among college teachers who have not had much direct contact with foreign-born colleagues to grant them an *a priori* superiority in mental capacity, a wider range of information, a vaster possession of what is conveniently called "background." Not that the average European high school does not provide its pupils with a wider and more thorough training in solid disciplines than the average American secondary school; this is a commonplace that hardly needs repetition. But the commonplace has apparently, through long reiteration, sunk into the subconscious and there created an unexamined attitude of admiration and sometimes even awe. It is an occasionally embarrassing state of affairs, because (although I imagine that there may be foreign intellectuals who thrive on deftly handled name-dropping and the production of splendorous generalities that impose by their vastness rather than by profundity) in general one prefers being appreciated for what one is, rather than for seeming to represent Universal Culture or some such pomposity.

The danger of being mistaken in this way, however, is minimal in the genuinely scholarly world. The immigrant who is fortunate enough to live in an academic community is unlikely to be made the idol of misplaced hero worship. In a world where scepticism is one of the first working rules there is very little chance for the fake to pass unexposed. It is true that almost every campus has its legends about immigrant teachers—usually in the foreign language divisions—who came in the early decades of this century and have turned into figures of mirth for their students as well as their colleagues. Their linguistic slips or downright inadequacies, their ignorance of American ways or plain professional incompetence, lightened by charming touches of eccentricity, provide innumerable anecdotes for the coffee break or after-dinner talk. But everyone realizes that their academic merit lay only in speaking German or French as natives, while nobody ever took them seriously as scholars. "Characters" of this order can hardly subsist in a self-respecting English department, where mastery of a foreign language is only a secondary asset and where professional competence has to prove itself against a strong and keen competition.

In addition to the absence of hero worship, there is another "objective" reason why I am not aware of an opposition between immigrant and American environment. The scholar, especially if he works in the humanities, is trained to be at home in a variety of spiritual worlds other than his *hic et nunc.* If he had a good education in English literature, for example, he will have received some of the "feel" of a Germanic mead hall or an eighteenth-century London coffeehouse. He will be able to visualize and imaginatively live on the road to Canterbury in the 1380's, peep into a Victorian blackening factory, or roam the woods at Walden Pond. To re-create in his imagination worlds of the past that are utterly different from his own in manners, dress, language, beliefs, and customs, is an exercise on which a good deal of his professional activity—teaching as well as scholarship—rests. Indeed, to occupy oneself with a good novel, even with a single poem, usually means to penetrate into a world *sui generis,* and the better one can divest himself from his own ego and the accidents of his library, the better will his understanding of the literary work be. A person whose imagination is thus trained to live in different worlds will find it comparatively easy, perhaps unessential, to live in a country which is not his native land. Of course, imagination and reality, literature and life, are not the same, and a scholar would make a pitiable fool of himself if he equated his field of historical investigation or a work of art with the world of Coca-Cola vending machines. But somehow the conscientious research into fields that do not form part of one's immediate surroundings prepares the immigrant scholar's mind for a peculiar attitude to his new world.

Whatever this attitude may precisely be, it is not one of self-conscious opposition. Rather, it is one of scientific curiosity with the scientist's objectiveness replaced by sympathy. The literary scholar observes his concrete world, evaluates, and even criticizes it, but he will tend to do so with Coleridge's "suspension of disbelief." This attitude of detached interest is, again, a working rule he is expected to follow in research and criticism; but it may easily determine his way of experiencing the real life around him.

One can therefore say that the literary scholar carries with him as an acquired habit a certain universality of outlook which makes it relatively easy for him to be at home in a variety of cultures. This universality has, moreover, a very concrete form for the immigrant. Scholarship today has such a strong international basis that an immigrant scholar need hardly ever feel isolated in a foreign environment. Every major university in America has on its staff a variety of foreign-born professors or research fellows. Visiting lecturers and exchange scholars come and go in unending succession. Frequent professional meetings bring together colleagues from all over the world: during the past year and a half, for example, Cambridge, Massachusetts, and New York were the scenes of two international congresses of linguistics, modern languages and literatures. All this creates an atmosphere in which the local habitat assumes only secondary importance. This universality of scholarship is of course nothing new—scholars have always wandered. Whether the fact that today many of them flit to and fro is a healthy situation for productive thought does not concern us here; but it certainly lessens the feeling that countries and cultures are eons apart.

This is all well and good, one might now object; the immigrant scholar who works in the field of literature does then not experience himself as a foreign body in the living organism of his academic world. But what about American society at large? Surely he has to buy bread and milk at the supermarket, face inanities at PTA meetings where decisions about the intellectual health of his children are being made, and talk the used-car salesman into giving him a good deal. Is he not touched to the quick by the painful differences between his European background and values and those of the New World? He is. But here the professor of English (and the same is true of other humanities) finds himself in a peculiar position, because his shocks and frustrations, his indignant repulsions are shared to the fullest by his native American colleagues and students. Antagonism against the destruction of individual values and liberty by a technocratic mass society is not the property of immigrants only; it is the common reaction among what is perhaps not quite correctly called "the intellectuals" in America.

About ten years ago the French immigrant Henri Peyre, professor at Yale, spoke on "The Study of Literature" in a series of lectures about the European scholar in America. In the course of his essay he analyzed several deficiencies or fallacies in the American educational system which are most blatant to European professors, and finally made the suggestion that they "may be traced to the unconscious acceptance of two ideals by academic scholars and critics: the ideals of the businessman and of the scientist." (Perhaps Henri Peyre should have written "the technician.") From my experiences, however, I can only conclude that these ideals have not been accepted at all, consciously or unconsciously, by my colleagues who teach English literature. On the contrary, there is a general opposition to the techniques of modern salesmanship and its prostitution of language; to the utilitarian approach to learning and knowledge; to administrative tendencies to replace originality and individuality by a well-lubricated organizational machine; to the conformity in values and tastes of the masses. Most young English instructors are at very great pains to awaken their students' minds and sharpen their critical faculty. Criticism and satire of those dangers to individual freedom and creative thought has become fashionable: one has only to think of such best-sellers as *The Hidden Persuaders, The Organization Man*, and *The Status Seekers*. It even seems at times that American graduate students and young college teachers are actually less able than their foreign-born colleagues to take the threats of Madison Avenue or cybernetics with a grain of salt. The point, however, is that in this respect the immigrant scholar finds himself on a common front with his American fellow scholars in defense of values which are not exclusively those of his native *patrie*.

The specific "fallacies" which Henri Peyre analyzed in his essay are of course very real and cause much complaint from everyone concerned. Professor Peyre mentioned the general fondness for innovation, the requirement that scholars and teachers produce intensively, and the ubiquitous bad writing (by which he was primarily thinking of pseudo-scientific jargon). Of the three, the second deserves a little closer attention. It is quite true that a heavy demand lies on all American scholars to publish—articles, books, lectures, addresses, anything that will go on the yearly departmental bibliography. The first-rate scholar who has been fortunate enough during his dissertation work to hit upon a mine of unexplored material will not be bothered by such pressure. But his equally intelligent and sensitive friend whose subject simply needs a longer period of gestation is thereby driven into a frantic haste whose outcome can only be a premature or decidedly third-rate work. Again, it is not only the immigrant scholar who notices the evil; he probably suffers less under it than his American colleague. Once more he finds himself in league with a wide resentment against an unhealthy pressure, whether it comes from his departmental chairman, the university administration, or the abstract notion behind both that the faculty has to show "achievements" to the tax-paying public.

In all these matters, then, the rift is not between immigrant scholar and American life, especially university life, but rather between teachers in the humanities and outside forces that do not share, or are perhaps hostile to, humanistic values. Nowhere is this rift more clearly defined than in the attitudes toward the ideals of education. It is perhaps presumptuous to speak of educational ideals in America. The school system is so diversified that one should not generalize. Aims and goals are, as is well known, decided upon individually by each separate unit: school districts, universities, the various groups of private schools, and so on. Yet the public schools do represent the largest sector of education, and they are staffed by a fairly homogeneous group of men and women—mostly women—who were trained in state teachers' colleges and schools of education. If they received any "ideals" of education at all, those ideals seem to be a series of the vaguest, too much repeated commonplaces. If they share one common goal, it is to make boys and girls into good citizens—the emphasis lies on the socializing function of public schools, not on imparting knowledge or developing thought or fostering creativity.

This sociological outlook of contemporary educators is one of the barriers that alienate them deeply from scholars and teachers in the humanities. Another is the noticeably lower scholastic standards held to in departments of education. They prove a considerable stumbling block to any education student who takes a course in another department, as well as to the teacher who has to deal with him. A third barrier is the abuse of the English language which one finds so frequently in textbooks and the technical literature on education. Clichés, meaningless strings of abstract nouns, unnecessary and ugly neologisms are all aspects of a language that frequently throws the mantle of glittering verbiage over the most ordinary triviality. For this lingo a generally accepted term has been found: educationalese, and college freshmen are warned against it by their English Composition instructors as a prime example of bad writing. All this, I think, shows clearly enough the awareness on the part of, not just foreign scholars, but English departments in general, of the deficiencies in contemporary American education. There is a split in values and a good deal of hidden, though well-realized, scorn between the humanities and Schools of Education.

If the immigrant scholar has little occasion for feeling alone and separated from his environment, then his convictions, his general intellectual outlook, scholarly productivity and effectiveness in the classroom can hardly be hampered by the fact of his having been born and educated abroad. It is of course essential that he master the language fairly well and that he have a cultivated sensitivity for the literature and poetry written in a foreign language. And even with regard to his mastery of the language it must be pointed out how admirably tolerant and generous American colleges and students are, even to the point of being quite unreasonable. Thus it has happened more than once that exchange students from Europe and the Far East with a totally insufficient command of English were employed to teach freshman science classes where the students did their best to stick it out rather than rise in protest. The great tolerance in accepting the foreign teacher without question becomes manifest to me at the beginning of every semester when after a week of class meetings no more than two or three smart students come up to inquire about my origins, because my accent does not sound quite

American to them. Beyond this brief inquiry there is never any further pertinent reaction.

Likewise, I do not think that the fact of being an immigrant hampers scholarly productivity. A number of European scholars who came to America in the 1930's expressed apprehension in this regard when they compared—perhaps somewhat nostalgically —the relative ease and leisure of a professor's life in their native country with the hectic busyness here. I cannot judge the leisure at European universities before 1930; but it seems that today the Ordinarius for, let us say, Modern German Literature at Heidelberg or Göttingen has much less free time for research and scholarly writing than a professor of English or American literature does at one of the forty or fifty highest-ranking American universities. Similarly, editors of European learned journals are by no means as overwhelmingly flooded with articles submitted for publication as their colleagues in this country are. And I do not think there is a noticeable difference in the quality of published scholarly or critical papers.

If there are, thus, very few negative factors that impede the fruitful activity of the foreign-born professor of English, does he, on his part, have anything positive to contribute to his profession for which he is better suited than his American colleague? During the past thirty years immigrant scholars have contributed much to the various sectors of intellectual and academic life in America. The stimulus and methodological influence of a linguist like Roman Jakobson or of literary critics like Leo Spitzer and René Wellek have been far-reaching and, although none of these men is or was working in an English department, have been felt by a large number of graduate students in English. If I may be personal once more, I would like to point out, in the following, some larger directions in which I believe the immigrant scholar can make his most fruitful contribution, especially in a humanistic field like English literature.

First, an insistence on serious learning and scholarship. The nineteenth-century German notion that language and literature, history, and even the fine arts should be studied as *Wissenschaften* is a most fertile idea whose possibilities have as yet not been fully realized. I would by no means advocate a return to mere fact-gathering, to arid source study for its own sake, or to the biographical method as the only salutary way to the interpretation of a poem. What I would emphasize is the spirit of disciplined truth-seeking that infused the giant scholars of the past century. All too often one runs into graduate students and college professors who have chosen an academic career because their conception of it promised them a gentleman's life of leisure pleasantly filled with aesthetic delights and sophisticated cocktail parties. Most of them, fortunately, drop out in time, but a few stay on to produce lectures and articles that drip with subjective impressions or sparkle with intellectual pyrotechnics in which scholarly methods or critical writing have become ends in themselves. In this respect America simply lacks a strong tradition of scholarship, an image of the scholar as a man who is passionately committed to truth and willing to sacrifice comforts and pleasures. Although a good many English scholars in this country fully represent this image in their lives and work, their influence on English studies and students at large has been rather small.

The situation is even worse in regard to our primary and secondary education. Despite all the complaints issued in the last decade, high-school students remain ill prepared for genuine university work. The nervous spasm that ran through the American school world on the occasion of Sputnik has given way to the former quiet and complacency. Apparently, nothing will be done by the high schools to replace courses in social behavior and safe driving with serious intellectual disciplines. The college professor therefore has to accept the fact that, by and large, truly higher education (in European terms) tends more and more to begin in graduate school. While there is nothing theoretically wrong in stretching out the formative process a few years, in practice the current situation does present a picture of wasted time and lost opportunities. For most normally gifted persons it is virtually impossible to acquire a genuine proficiency in two or three foreign languages or to memorize lists of cut-and-dried historical dates after the age of twenty-five. Everyone agrees that without a ready grasp of concrete facts understanding is impossible, and a reading knowledge of foreign languages as well as a framework of the relevant past history is essential for the advanced study of literature. I must confess that I am often amazed at the chasm between the general ignorance of undergraduate students and the impressive knowledge of good graduates; it is only fair to the latter to praise the zeal and hard work with which they try to make up for past deficiencies. Nevertheless, the weaknesses of secondary education remain.

As I have hinted earlier, these weaknesses derive largely from an overemphasis in current American educational thought on the socializing aspect of education, on the goal of preparing good citizens. How to get along with one's fellow men is so much in the foreground of our educators' attention that they have little time to consider how to get along with oneself—that part of life seems relegated mostly to the psychiatrist's couch. The danger in this more and more sociological approach to education is not so much that individual personalities are deformed and stunted in their growth, as that it prepares the way to the coming of a totalitarian society. Even in the alternative to totalitarianism which is so much discussed today, the pluralistic society, the individual figures merely as a member of a group. In this engulfing pressure of social forces to conform, the voices that would uphold the value of the human individual and cry out for the air needed to develop individual potentialities are few and rather powerless. Old-fashioned humanists are passed over as eggheads who are completely out of touch with reality; religion for most Americans means "good fellowship"; and the late attempt to protest against all this, the movement of the Beatniks (tellingly enough clothed in beards and sandals—the emblems of the true man of God), has been obviously too petty and odd from the start to produce any deep effects.

Here the study of literature (including drama in its various forms, from the legitimate theater to TV) seems to be a most promising means to lead young minds to a consideration of what man is, and to compel them—gently yet persistently—to seek for an answer by themselves. This use of literature is not a new idea. The great poems written in the dawn of Western literature, the *Iliad* and the *Odyssey*, were used by the ancient Greeks for centuries as models of what a noble man is and does. If today we do not have a unique and universally binding ideal image of man, expressed either in theory or in literature, we can at least use the latter to enrich experience, to sharpen sensitivities, and to make students think.

The role of the immigrant English professor in this under-taking is a humble one. Essentially he will find himself in league with a good many fellow teachers. What he can contribute to the common effort is a broader outlook and a deeper personal experience, which might carry greater conviction. With his intimate knowledge of at least one foreign language he is at home in more than one culture and hence, unless he is intellectually blind or dishonest, immune to any narrow-minded nationalism. His approach to ideals and works will necessarily be more universal; he is more capable of taking Goethe and Schiller as well as Henry Adams and Walt Whitman *cum grano salis*.

This universality has, further, not only an international but also a historical dimension. Literary scholars in general still share a familiarity with the tastes, beliefs, and sentiments of past ages, despite the tendency in some English departments to allow their graduate students an early specialization in contemporary American or British literature. By and large, the Ph.D. in English is still less a-historically-minded than intellectuals in other disciplines. But the immigrant scholar has a clear advantage over them all insofar as he spent his formative years in a world where the past survives. It is often said that European children grow up among the physical remains of the Middle Ages, if not of ancient Greece and Rome. In the case of an intellectually alert adolescent, however, traditions survive and are imbedded—as it were, by osmosis—in much subtler forms. Not only do castles and cathedrals reflect a dead past to him, but in institutions, folk customs, and richly diversified societies that have not gone through the melting pot the past continues to live. To a well-educated European, Attic democracy and scholasticism, Virgil and St. Augustine, Manicheism and Rousseau, the Reformation and monastic culture, are not so many names and abstractions, but types of human experience which form part of his cultural inheritance and, in very curious ways, truly part of himself.

In utilizing and handing on this living experience of mankind's past, I believe, lies the greatest possible contribution the immigrant scholar can make. By this, of course, I do not mean the nostalgic praise of bygone Golden Ages or the withdrawal into an ivory tower of antiquarianism. We all have to face the present and occasionally think of the future. But to do so with an awareness that man began to live, love, make mistakes, and think about these experiences many centuries before 1776 may be a great help in finding one's way in an age that demands new answers. Let me mention, by way of example, one contemporary problem of very wide scope in whose solution such an awareness may be of practical consequence. Political theorists seem to be agreed that in the near future some kind of world government will emerge in which the presently hostile power blocks will be carefully balanced and will, so it is hoped, peacefully coexist. Exactly what such an organization will look like and how it can be achieved, we do not know. The political experience of recent years, however, has made it evident that simply pouring out monetary aid to underprivileged countries or bestowing, with self-applauding airs, a democratic government on nations that are not yet ready for it, entails failure. More than that is needed: understanding, primarily, and an appreciation of the idiosyncrasies, the historical achievement, and the culture of other nations. To foster such attitudes is a task wherein no one could be more effective than a person in whom historical knowledge and objectivity are combined with direct personal experience of different cultures. While it would be facetious to consider himself as another Jonas or as a modern parallel to the Greek scholars who, after 1451, carried Antiquity to the West, the immigrant scholar of our days realizes that his peculiar situation offers him opportunities and even challenges to make a contribution of his very own.

DANIEL KUBAT

Theory of the Visiting Scholar

DISCIPLES IN SEARCH OF MASTERS were observed journeying to places of higher learning from the time of the establishment of the *universitas scholarium* in Bologna, if not before.
The great proliferation of universities toward the close of the
Middle Ages brought about problems of "cross-cultural exchange" which, if realized on a campus of, say, a large state
university, would make the American students numerically negligible. The lingua franca no doubt contributed greatly to the
facility of social intercourse, but, being taken for granted, as is
American English on our campuses, it was not considered to be
a major factor in the success or failure of the body of scholars
assembled at a particular place. No doubt, ethnic exodus now
and then resulted in the founding of a new university by a dis-
senting group; on the whole, however, the visiting scholars,
being primarily students of advanced learning, did pretty well
at the institutions where their calling chanced to take them. In
the jolly socializing in pubs and houses of diverse repute, no
doubt brawls were sometimes the order of the day and the quar-
reling students more likely than not aligned themselves along
ethnic lines, to use today's phrase. The purpose of their presence
was not the *universitas* as togetherness but the *universitas* as a
guild of students, of masters; as a union, we can say, to fend off
the conflicting interests of the community within whose walls
they all had to live as foreign bodies, as strangers. Once having
established their identity as strangers, however stigmatized on
occasions, since not all communities were fond of having old
established ways disrupted by strange customs and ways of life,
they became unified by their pursuit of available learning.

With the decline of the feudal social order, which ran across
ethnic boundaries, and with the emergence of nation states,

learning became more nationalistic. People began to speak about German philosophy, the French legal mind, or Italian aesthetics as if these were attributes of a national character. The nationalism nourished in home universities did bring forth some traits peculiar to each system, as would be the case with vicinal and mental isolation anywhere. The resulting aberrations which brought forth World War II—and which, no doubt, still survive in places not fully accessible to strangers—should have taught the world a lesson on the detriments of cultural isolation under conditions of industrial civilization.

Students of different nationalities and origins have always been found on the Left Bank in Paris, on the streets of Heidelberg, in the colleges of Oxford, or in the dark halls of the Carolinum in Prague. They were either too few to be noticed, sufficiently independent to be no problem, or so well adapted as to disappear among the many. Mainly, however, they were accepted for what they were, whether they came to learn or just to polish their gentlemanly demeanor. And problems of financial dependency, when they arose, as with the refugees after World War I, were dealt with by competent agencies.

In all the places to which the students came—places resplendent, colorful, intriguing, respectable, demure, noisy or quiet, small or large—the university quarter was the hub of things. The townspeople were either friendly or not so friendly, but they never required from the residing scholars any particular commitment to the country whose guests they were or to the university system within which they learned or to the people whom they met on their daily errands. Even after World War II, this remained essentially true in places like Munich, or Strasbourg, or Copenhagen, or Cambridge.

The United States has for a long time exported its own students, who studied in Madrid, in Rome, but mainly in Paris and Heidelberg and London. It was not until after World War II that the United States rose to the coveted position of international leadership which attracted the attention of prospective visiting scholars to a country which by its own efforts had become so great. Today, tens of thousands of foreign students from all parts of the world come to the United States to live perhaps for a year or two and to learn perhaps for life. Their numbers are not staggering when compared to the numbers of the native Americans on the campuses. But it is their status as foreign students—as visiting scholars, if you will—which invites us to think about this very old, yet somehow, now very new tradition. Is it perhaps that we, as Americans, feel too much like newcomers ourselves to be put into the position of guardians of knowledge? Perhaps what we have to offer to foreign learners seems too freshly imported and too naïvely handled. Perhaps our rituals of handling knowledge are those of the *nouveaux riches*, full of exuberant gaudiness.

Lawrence Durrell believes in the ambience of a landscape which permeates its inhabitants. One either is able to sense the landscape or is not. It would be difficult to validate such an insight empirically; but in something of the same way, I think, one can believe in the ambience of a learned landscape, which permeates its inhabitants. There are various ways in which people handle learning, ideas, knowledge: one can imagine some shoveling notions; others playing dominoes with concepts, mechanically, albeit accurately with no gross errors of logic; and still others, although functionally illiterate, serene against the backdrop of rich cultural traditions. All this, obviously, may be only in the eyes of the observer, but it is the observer who matters to us if we are to discuss the case of the modern visiting scholar in the United States.

To construct a theory of visiting scholars, one could proceed, according to custom, from a systematic observing of phenomena (visiting scholars) to an abstraction of certain characteristic behavioral traits in certain regularly occurring settings, thus arriving at verifiable sets of propositions about the observed phenomena (visiting scholars). In this essay, however, we shall spare ourselves such empirical drudgery. Rather we shall postulate from the lack of certain observed phenomena the desirability of certain characteristic behavioral traits (not presently occurring) which might occur were the settings more propitious. To put it in a more acceptable language: having found a damaged skull of Homo sapiens, we shall try to reconstruct the posture of the whole skeleton. Such a procedure is quite common among physical anthropologists. There is no reason to believe that a cultural anthropologist should not be able to reconstruct the posture of a visiting scholar from incomplete information on the behavior of some foreign student at one school or another.

It is undoubtedly true that a traveler can be treated as a stranger only in places of permanent social order. If this is so, what can we call those foreign journeymen who come in thousands to the American universities? The implication of this query is, of course, that the temporary environs of the foreign student in the United States is not conducive to his being considered a stranger. If he were so considered, the rules of coming and going would be defined quite clearly, and travel on well-marked roads of social encounter should not elicit any comments other than "How interesting," or perhaps "How exotic!"

The egalitarian spirit of an American college and university campus disdains deference to foreign students and discourages condescension. This ideology puts the visiting learner in a difficult position: although there is a conscientious effort not to discriminate against him (any racial discrimination is usually based on color, not on nationality), the foreign student, who by his very past is unlike the others whom he converses with, is encouraged to be like them; he in turn often tries to fulfill this expectation to become one of the many because he, like other humans, cannot tolerate unstructured situations.

In the early days of foreign study, there was no problem; foreign students were considered and treated as strangers on the American campus. As their numbers have increased, however, their place has become less well defined, and internationally-minded foundations and agencies have undertaken studies to determine the impact and consequences of large-scale foreign student exchange. One among such groups, the Social Science Research Council, appointed a Committee on Cross-Cultural Studies to sponsor and co-ordinate research on foreign students on American campuses. The research would be exploratory in nature, depicting the life adjustment of several culturally contrasting nationality groups (phase one of the program) to life in America and, afterward, back at home; systematic studies (phase two of the program) would follow up problems and hypotheses unearthed in phase one. Four exploratory studies were published on the Indian, Swedish, Mexican, and Japanese students (and scholars) between 1956 and 1958. Three systematic studies were done, dealing with academic and social adjustment, national status perception and adjustment, and attitudes and social relations.*

The findings of the studies are neither startling nor unexpected. Academic adjustment and performance of the foreign students were positively related to their facility in English, to the recognition of their academic credits from their home countries, and to their acceptance of American academic practices. In general, the foreign students' liking of their American experience followed a U-shaped curve: excitement over the sojourn at the onset, disillusionment with certain adverse traits of American life after about a half a year of exposure, and finally a more balanced acceptance and positive evaluation of the total experience in America, either at the end of the stay or after their return home. Those students who came to the United States mostly for experience proved to be the most successful adapters; those who came strictly for professional training were, in the main, not as happy with their social life, although they valued the professional training open to them.

Those students were quite happy with their sojourn who either considered the American campus situation flexible or who had a good measure of personal adaptability and thus enjoyed a good measure of exposure to the style of American life. This indicated that skills of communication can overcome any initial status discrepancies resulting from invidious evaluation of national origins. If successful social relations of the foreign students with their American counterparts are the measure of positive

* The series of seven volumes was published by the University of Minnesota Press:

  Richard D. Lambert, and Marvin Bressler. *Indian Students on an American Campus*. 1956.

  Franklin D. Scott. *The American Experience of Swedish Students*. 1956.

  Ralph L. Beals, and Norman D. Humphrey. *No Frontier to Learning*. 1957.

  John H. Bennett, Herbert Passin, and Robert K. Knight. *In Search of Identity*. 1958.

  Richard T. Morris (with the assistance of Oluf M. Davidsen). *The Two Way Mirror*. 1960.

  William H. Sewell, and Oluf M. Davidsen. *Scandinavian Students on an American Campus*. 1961.

  Claire Selltiz, June R. Christ, Joan Havel, and Stuart W. Cook. *Attitudes and Social Relations of Foreign Students in the United States*. 1963.

attitudes to the United States, then European students showed more cultural affinity than non-Europeans; this may, of course, be only a measure of sophistication, since European students are generally more traveled than non-Europeans. On the whole, the findings show that those students whose primary purpose was to have a cross-cultural experience felt all in all very satisfied with their stay and returned home happy, having seen another people immersed in happiness. These students showed the greatest degree of social adjustment and acculturation to their temporary environment, having been *Romani Romae*. Those students who came to the United States to pursue a particular field of learning scored, on the whole, lower on the adjustment (i.e., happiness) measure.

The disconcerting part of these studies is the assumptions which underlie them. It is quite unfortunate that the ideology of cross-cultural student exchange is directed by the supposition that personal adjustment take precedence over intellectual excellence. The over-all measures of success or failure of the student exchange program seem to be couched in the imagery of "one big happy family." "If the student is not particularly unfavorable toward Americans or America, but seems deeply dissatisfied with his stay here, . . . one reason may be that his chief source of dissatisfaction is lack of contact with Americans— inability to make friends with Americans or to see a variety of American life" (Morris, p. 141). Or, heaven forbid, he may have overconcentrated on his studies, which would have, of course, cut down his chances of cross-cultural contact. These measures of happiness with one's stay in a foreign country, namely the frequency of personal intercourse, are considered important despite the collateral findings that most foreign students resent the shallowness of interpersonal relations. It would have been perhaps more significant to devise measures of cross-cultural discourse which would evaluate intellectual sharing and appreciation rather than degree of chumminess. Discourse is by nature argumentative and probing, a process of establishing respect among intellectual adversaries. It defines the boundaries of one's identity and thus the recognition of the discoursing partners as separate entities. Who knows, perhaps this voluntary *Gleichs- haltung* of the campus life brings forth the search for identity among the social fringes of the student body. And it seems to a casual observer that the foreign students on American campuses are quite often seen hanging out with this fringe, another aspect which the studies failed to appreciate.

So far our case of the infracted skull. It is often assumed that our perception of the role of the foreign students on our campuses differs from the perception a resident of Budapest would have of, let us say, the students from the Somali Republic. This hypothetical resident might view the presence of the Somali students at the local university either with love and devotion, although more likely with indifference, and, as some recent events have shown, with some enmity, since the scarce commodities are more accessible to students with foreign currency than to the local residents. Similarly, local residents in an American college town are not greatly excited about or enthralled with the foreign students in their communities. In both places the foreign students may come to the attention of the residents of the community only when, following their own cultural habits, they violate local practices; European students, for example, are likely to wonder at the rigidly regulated association of the sexes in living quarters.

International policies of the respective countries are more likely to influence the situation and study conditions for the foreign students. The Soviet countries have aims in matters of educational exchange similar to ours in the United States, namely, to convey the idea of the superiority of our respective social systems. Both parties are newcomers to the international limelight, but their educational systems are somewhat diverse. Whereas Soviet education is trying to convey to students a substantial amount of information on ideologically immune academic disciplines and in that manner treats the natives and foreign visitors alike, our American educational system provides to the students far more ideologically sensitive information enveloped in a moral splendor, to use a slightly poetic expression. Whereas the Soviets then, having to coax foreign students via various privileges, specialize in students from countries distinctly in need, our aim seems to be to provide a sort of moral re-armament. It is true, of course, that after World War II we were involved in bringing over students from countries exposed to anti-democratic governments with the explicit purpose of re-educating them politically. This in itself was a worthwhile task. On the other hand, we know that social institutions once begotten have a very tenacious capacity for survival. The old ghost of the foreign student exchange program, expanded to several multiples of its original scope, still lingers on until today, when quite a few incoming students do not need or desire this particular political re-education which once was helpful. Besides, we should not forget that the melting pot attitude is still quite strong in our country; we seem reluctant to consider anyone our equal until he becomes like one of us. This attitude, I think, is responsible for our inclination to treat any foreign visitor as an immigrant. We are likely to be surprised to hear that a foreign visitor wants to return to his home country instead of staying in this country. Since our case study was drawn from material collected almost ten years ago, one may hope that conditions have changed to allow students to remain primarily students rather than potential subjects of political indoctrination.

Having digressed, necessarily I think, to see the political superstructure which brought about the peculiarly American approach to visiting scholars, it is time to expand the findings in our case study to reconstruct a posture of the visiting scholar. A few of the findings on foreign students in America were, as we remember, that they became better adapted to American life the better they spoke the language and the less they were interested in acquiring specialized training. In other words, those who came here just to improve their gentlemanly (or ladylike) demeanor did so, although one might argue that an exposure to various sophisticated haunts in New York City, for instance, would have accomplished more. On the other hand, those whose main interest was absorption of as much specialized information as possible did not exhibit jovial behavior, no doubt in direct violation of Benthamian invectives.

When we get two divergent and not very meaningful results of an educational program which in its goals depends on the insights of Socrates but in its means leans heavily on the advice of the Athenian sophists, and when such a program becomes a host to foreign visitors, then perhaps we should seek for a further explanation. It may be we have measured only the explicit goals of the foreign student program; the goals being misdirected, we may have obtained an accurate measure of the misdirection, a knowledge in itself very valuable. Assuming that this is true, then what is the explanation and what, optimistically, are the remedies for such misdirection? And what, ultimately, is the real status of a visiting scholar?

If it is true that human beings do not tolerate unstructured situations well, how does this affect the problem of the visiting scholars? We have noticed before that social customs, if reasonably ingrained and localized, make those who journey through the area socially visible. Such a situation may invite generous hospitality, if there is enough to share, or may invite ostracism and mistrust if there has been reason earlier to find dissatisfaction with the transients. We also assume as well proven by those competent in behavioral research that, under the ideology of equality, groups exert pressure to "equalize" their members and that the pressures, for a while at least, are strongest on those who are most different but still defined as members of the groups. Hence the finding that the foreign students' exposure to American life was greater in smaller colleges. Had we assumed that social inequality is a sign of a greater sophistication in the division of labor (and knowledge), exchange of information about the different customs and ways of life would follow with a greater detachment and with less pressure toward alikeness. Now, an American campus is more "structured" in terms of scheduling of events and daily routine than most of the campuses from which our visitors come. But this aspect of academic and social schedule is not really what constitutes a structured or an unstructured situation for a visiting scholar. In all likelihood he is going to be amazed at the things he is supposed to do, the schedules he is supposed to follow, the assumption that he is not self-reliant and that he needs institutional crutches to go about his tasks of learning. But what actually remains bypassed and unscheduled and unspecified is his personal status as a human being, a foreigner with past experiences, coming perhaps from those landscapes ambient in a rich cultural heritage. We seem to accord the visiting scholar (the incipient one in particular) a zero status rank and value him later according to the degree in which he resembles us; such an attitude, no doubt, caters to our demiurgical needs.

The notion of equality, which we naïvely tend to confound with pity—in itself a virtue—de-emphasizes excellence, which is a part of many an educational system from which our visiting scholars derive. When the rules of the war are well known and the dueling brings forth the victor, somebody gets wounded; the honorable victor, nonetheless, shakes hands with the adversary. Our business world, where excellence is measured by more tangible means, has retained some of its original competitive spirit and has ritualized the failures through bankruptcy proceedings. In our academic competition we seem to lack ritualized bankruptcy proceedings, perhaps to the detriment of the academic cause. That does not mean that we do not fail students or that we as scholars do not fail ourselves. Rather, it means that failure is associated with disgrace. Since this is true, then our efforts seem to be concentrated more on the prevention of failure than on the furthering of success; in the academic world, therefore, we tend to view education as a remedial business with everybody included and often have little energy left to pursue excellence. Now all this, oversimplified though it obviously is, should prompt us to ask whether the exchange of incipient scholars or mature ones is justified when the conditions of competitive excellence do not prevail.

Ever since the emergence of nationalist scholarship, the visitors to places of higher learning from neighboring countries have been at a slight disadvantage. Whereas the purpose of the visiting sojourn is to exchange ideas, the medium of exchange is necessarily foreign to the foreigners. Usually, no doubt, the visiting scholar and student have familiarized themselves readily with the prevailing language, although difficulties of linguistic precision in verbal disputes are not hard to imagine. I would think that the lingua franca of the Middle Ages provided the possibility of establishing a proper status relationship between two discoursing scholars, eliminating thus the involuntary paternalistic attitude on the part of the discourse opponent whose native language was being used. To reconstruct the status of a medieval visiting scholar, we would say that a lingua franca was important to the flourishing of wandering scholars, if we may slightly abuse this term. In modern times, however, any of the current languages may serve this purpose, and do on many an occasion, as long as the discoursing parties consider the use of a particular language on agreement and not a prerogative. In the case of American higher learning, it is by no means negligible that monoglotism makes a virtue out of necessity.

In our case study it has been pointed out that academic success—or rather non-failure—is closely associated with proficiency in the language and with the time devoted to study; on the other hand, it has been noted that an overconcentration on studies may lead the student, or the visiting scholar, to forfeit cross-cultural enjoyment. This conclusion is based on the apparent assumption that a pursuit of learning is entirely separate from everyday life. The previous discussion of ambient academic landscapes suggests itself in this context. I would argue that being engrossed as a visiting scholar in a discussion—oral or written—with the foremost exponents of one's discipline in a foreign country should tell the visitor more about the country than a sequence of coffees, mixers, and picnics. After all, human habits in devouring food resemble one another a bit more than habits of intellectual discourse. If the specialized knowledge of a discipline were really international, what justification is there for this traveling of visiting scholars? If, however, it is not international and if an exposure to landscapes is what matters, then the *raison d'être* of visiting scholars is preserved.

What we have been discussing at some length is essentially the Socratic notion of higher education as reaching into the soul of things as contrasted with the sophists' idea of a man as educated if he is able to utilize his factual knowledge of human behavior successfully in the manner of Dale Carnegie. The humanist notion of erudition represented the same sporting of knowledge to facilitate social intercourse—in a quite different environ, to be sure—as does our teaching of social graces to get along well in social life. These graces, which no doubt are almost a national characteristic when extended to the visiting scholars, tend to mislead them into assuming a more ready social and personal acceptance than is really the case. Perhaps a simulation of restraint toward those who are guests would be a step in countering the almost inevitable accusation of Americans as shallow people, which they really are not. While we are well versed in certain mechanisms of social encounter, the fact that we really seldom understand them may, and often does, lead to misunderstandings in cross-cultural realms.

Thus, from the observed failings of the cross-cultural student exchange and the perhaps not so fortunate emphasis of the program, we have been able to suggest some principles which lend stature to those who chance to be visiting to share knowledge, the visiting scholars. The old institution of journeying from place to place to immerse oneself into the ambience of a learned landscape can be well maintained if we suspend our need to hover lovingly above the guest of honor and instead render to him his right to a unique social identity by treating him as a stranger in his own right. In exchange, we shall get recognition as intellectual peers or superiors according to our merits. If the visitors then choose to be remade in our own image, we can rightly claim it to our credit.

Peroration

THE RULES OF ACADEMIC COMPOSITION demand that a book should end with conclusions and leave the reader with a clear summary of the theses it chooses to announce. In the present case, however, it is not easy to satisfy the rule; the recapitulation of eleven individual arguments on just as many personal propositions appears as an act of dare. For help amidst the difficulties I had better turn to that old master of composition, Noah Webster, who once upon a time placed an *American Spelling Book* in the hands of the country's youngsters, sold it in a few million copies, and shaped with it the spelling, thinking, character, and morality of the nation more than all the colleges in the land. His Speller had crudely printed pages with woodcuts and fables—the fox and the grapes, the dog that kept bad company, the boy who stole apples, the milkmaid who spilled the milk—each of them teaching a "Moral." Schoolmaster Webster was a faithful son of Connecticut Puritans with that broad view that could take in at once the whole world from the English Channel to the Pacific Ocean. In his Preface to the Speller, written in 1782 or so, he tossed aside the parochial pedagogy of the following pages and with a broad sweep of view adjudged his home against the background of Europe. This was his judgment:

> Europe is grown old in folly, corruption, and tyranny. In that country laws are perverted, manners are licentious, literature is declining, and human nature is debased. For America in her infancy to adopt the present maxims of the old world would be to stamp the wrinkles of decrepit age upon the bloom of youth and to plant the seeds of decay in a vigorous constitution. American glory begins to dawn at a favorable period, and under flattering circumstances. We have the experience of the whole world before our eyes; but to receive indiscriminately the maxims of government, the manners and literary taste of Europe, and make them the ground on which to build our systems in America, must soon convince us that a durable and stately edifice can never be erected upon the mouldering pillars of antiquity.

Reading these lines of classical American English, I cannot resist the temptation of applying them to our times. The Europe of our century, the ghost-haunted castle where our civilization was born, the old continent of national and social hatred that I have seen in my youth, is grown old in folly, corruption, and tyranny. Yet, one should not be unjust and single out Europe just because one loves her more than the rest of the continents. The amount of folly, corruption, and tyranny is no less in Africa, Asia, or any other part of the world where the underdeveloped nations dwell. In this respect there is no difference between old continent and new continent; our globe as a whole is grown old in folly. America has the experience of the whole world before her eyes; so how does she select the suitable maxims, manners, and taste out of the global folly?

The help that the *American Spelling Book* can give me is not yet exhausted. On an October afternoon in 1836 the Transcendental Club of Boston met in the poorly furnished parlor of Bronson Alcott and discussed the topic: "American Genius—the Causes which Hinder Its Growth Giving Us no First-Rate Productions." We do not know what was said about this topic on that occasion when a marvelous sample of the American Genius gathered in the small parlor; as for the foibles of human nature, they might have discussed personal complaints on not being appreciated enough. But one authority asserts that Alcott recited Webster's Preface which he had known by heart since his school days. Alcott recited it, and one of the guests, Emerson, listened attentively because he was already mentally composing *The American Scholar* to be delivered ten months later as the Phi Beta Kappa Day Address.

What the gentlemen decided about the American Genius, Emerson never told us. But, as a result of that discussion, some of Noah Webster went into Emerson's *American Scholar*, perhaps nothing more than a vague allusion or just a random similarity that kindred souls often show without recognizing the ties of their spiritual kinship. I am particularly struck by one passage of Emerson which seems to give the transcendentalist response to Webster. "If the single man," Emerson declared, "plant himself indomitably upon his instincts, and there abide, the huge world will come round to him. Patience—patience;

with the shades of all the good and great for company; and for solace the perspective of your own infinite life; and for work the study and the communication of principles, the making of those instincts prevalent, the conversion of the world."

The imagination of Emerson was needed to connect such distant notions as the single man with his instincts and the conversion of the world, but here they were as integrated parts of the Emersonian philosophy ready to stir up an intellectual revolution in Massachusetts. The revolution subsided in time and helped to rejuvenate New England; but the words of Emerson have stayed with us and are as meaningful and lively now as on that August day at Cambridge when they had been delivered. The single man planting himself upon his instincts, working on the study and the communication of principles—this is the American scholar, native born or immigrant, past or present. But what about the conversion of the world in which he is supposed to have some part?

One point that the essays collected here make is this: that the era of tribal wisdom and national scholarship has forever passed; that there are no more wise men of the Orient, no gurus, yogis, shamans who would know what other wise men do not know; that, all the follies and divisiveness of the world notwithstanding, there is only one scholarship for all nations and all languages. The physicists speak the same language whether they use Chinese or English, and the psychologists grapple with the same problem whether they work in Norway or in the Congo. There is only one knowledge in which all nations must share, there is only one academe which must serve five continents. Let us not be deceived by tribal follies; we, mankind had better settle down to the work of building up the one unified and general campus that will teach and produce the same knowledge for all men.

If there is a second point that the present essays make, this must be a claim that America has taken great steps toward establishing the united scholarship of mankind. She has invited the learned men from all countries and given them new homes that they may regard as their own. Every year she would send out her sons to all countries and receive the sons of the same countries for common study and enquiry. Behold the congregation of her scholars, native born and immigrant: they have begun to convert the world of tribal lore into a united campus of learning.

Her national venture is still in its very beginnings, grappling with the initial uncertainties and experimental mistakes that mar every beginning. The previous pages dwell upon many concrete points of shortcomings. The extent of their criticism reflects the temperament and experience of the individual author and the magnitude of the global enterprise. Even if the faults they find are many, those are mistakes made while realizing Emerson's dream.

At any rate, America can take criticism, even carping, and hold to her course. With the shades of all the good and great for company, she keeps her broad view, takes in the whole world and maintains her belief in the feasibility of one and undivided human knowledge. What she does is not a simple purchase of the best brainpower available on the international market, not a simple revival of the liberality of ancient Athens or Rome in accommodating philosophers from the provinces. The aim of her venture is more: the establishment of an epoch in mankind's history that bears the indelible imprint of America, the epoch of the American Genius in its productive age, the epoch of giving first-rate production as a part of American leadership.

She has made great steps, but the road is long. The conversion of the world requires the elimination of tribal prejudices, the end of global follies, and the opening of the one, unified, international campus. The final goal is far away and the obstacles, small and great, are beyond count. But Webster was a demanding taskmaster and Emerson a scrupulous visionary. Their disciples cannot set their aims lower than the advice: plant yourself indomitably upon your instincts and there abide, and the huge world will come round to you.

JOHN KOSA

Index

DUE